Arabic For Beginners:

50 short stories for language learners

Malik Selim

SPECIAL BONUS!

Want this bonus book for **FREE?**

Get **FREE**, unlimited access to it and all of my new books by joining the Fan Base!

SCAN/W YOUR CAMERA TO JOIN!

Table of contents

Introduction

Why are stories a good way to learn a language?

There is no question that a person may learn a language in many ways. Some of the recognized approaches include textbooks, lectures and examinations in the classroom. However, the approach is typically missed if we discuss stories in this collection or not extensively considered. Let me explain why stories can be an effective method for learning new languages.

The education system, our roots and our history as humans

Storytelling is our oldest form of communication. The first signs of any storytelling were found in the Pyrenees mountains, dating back to 15,000 to 13,000 BC. We as humans have used stories for entertainment, education, preserving culture and a lot more! It isn't easy to pass something or somewhere today where a story isn't told, whether in business, entertainment, politics etc. Take religion as an example. How do we study the lives of the prophets? We learn them through stories.

Do you not remember a time in school, where you were requested to read novels that would allow you to understand lessons about life? Do you remember being told dozens of stories as a child by your parents to teach you about the world? Not to get it twisted, though. Stories are not solely for kids. The Harvard Business School teaches business through case studies, which are stories of other businesses' successes and failures. Okay, you get the idea; we use stories to make the whole learning experience more effective.

The way our brain operates

Stories activate parts of our brains that are not generally engaged when we are learning through the presentation of cold facts and figures. The left temporal cortex, the frontal & parietal cortices and the auditory cortex are used for; learning languages, associating ideas, memory and attention spans.

When we learn a story, we merge two things. That rational information and experiential parts of the brain. This then forms neural connections; when it is repeated, it strengthens and ultimately results in longer-term memory. You see, the memory part is KEY! especially when it comes to learning the Arabic Language. It ultimately comes down to how many words you know and your ability to use them correctly in the proper context. Psychologist Jerome Bruner suggested that the human brain is 22x more likely to remember facts within a story. I think you get the point. Learning through stories is a potent cocktail of meaning, memory, and emotion, and it is significantly more beneficial than learning through plain facts, which are quickly forgotten.

Stories teach us the culture, help us with interaction and set us up for real-life situations.

Stories help you to do this in multiple ways:

- Stories have meaning. What we learn in a story has some purpose. Because of that, we are learning to communicate meaningfully from the very beginning.

- Unlike textbooks, which usually have long lists of words, every word that appears in stories appears in context. This is crucial for any beginner to grasp and understand. One word in the Arabic Language can have dozens of meanings, so the beginner must understand which words to use in what context.

- Stories keep you interested and engaged; this, in turn, will keep you more motivated to learn. Let's face it; nobody wants to go through hundreds and hundreds of pointless exercises!

- Stories teach us lessons about culture, and they also get an emotional reaction out of us. This helps to make the Language a more authentic part of our lives.

Chapter 1: Some reading tips

You will find that most people who are learning a new language, are reading in a completely wrong way! as a result of that, they believe that the reading is too hard and that they can't take any benefit from reading. For this reason, I want to give you a few tips to consider when reading the stories in this book and any Arabic texts that you may read in the future.

- Tip number #1: Choose material that is at your level. This tip is more so for when you complete this book and move onto other Arabic texts. As a complete beginner, who just about knows how to read and write, I have crafted perfectly balanced stories. I have tried my utmost best to provide stories that are not too difficult but have plenty of vocabulary and are easy to understand. After you have completed this book, don't think that you can pick up any Arabic book and begin to read, rather take it slow and progress with material that is at your level. I highly advise you to follow this book along with an Arabic series like Al Arabiya Bayna Yadayk. It has material that is also not very difficult to understand.

- Tip number #2 – Use contextual clues to help you before you start reading the stories. By this, read the English title of the story (ONLY the title) before you read the Arabic story. I say this because the title can help you guess what the story's content will be. If you have a solid idea about what you are about to read, it will be easier to follow its meaning whilst you are reading it.

- Tip number #3: Read the Arabic stories right the way through to the end, one at a time. Your aim should be to get through as many stories as you can in one sitting. Don't stop to look up words that will come later. Just focus on the gist of what it is that you are reading. If you do anything else, e.g. stop to look up the words or the grammar for that text, you are preventing yourself from reading large amounts. The big benefit of reading itself is what we know as "extensive reading", which is reading large amounts (in this case, as many stories as possible in one sitting) for fun. Develop a habit of reading for pleasure. That is how you will learn and benefit the most.

- Tip number #4: After you have read each story (without yet reading the English translation), try to summarize in your mind what it is that you just read. Who are the characters? What did they do? What did they say? Where did it take place? was there a cliffhanger? You are not required to spend a long time doing this, but this is very important because we don't bring our native level reading skills with us when we read in another language. We usually tend to read from the first word, then the second, etc., we just read words at a time, and we stop interpreting and following along with the "bigger picture" of what we are reading! There is no point in reading a story where you are so focused on the words that you don't know the plot. Try to summarize in your mind what you have read.

Chapter 2: How to benefit from the stories in this book

Enough rambling from me. Okay, you now know the benefits of stories when it comes to learning languages. But what is the most effective way to learn a language through a story? I will break this down for you in three simple steps.

Step 1 – The first thing you want to try and do is immerse yourself in the Language with the stories you will read and hear. Re-wind the audio as often as you need to grasp the pronunciation of the words and until you master the words. It's a simple step, really; you will read and listen, read and listen, read and listen, over and over again until you feel confident to move onto the next stage.

Bear in mind that in this first step, you want to push yourself and read without the English translations initially; as soon as you remove the translations, you are removing the struggle and the grit from the whole process. Immerse yourself in the sounds of the Language. Remember that the main goal in step 1 is not to "learn". We are simply immersing ourselves in the Language so that our brain can learn the Language, all by itself. By continuously pushing our brains to understand the story, even though it may be in a foreign language, we activate the parts of our brain that I discussed in the introduction. You will find that the more you read and the more you listen, your brain will start to understand and pick up more and more words. Remember that it's not about what we don't understand from the stories; rather, it's all about what your brain is learning to understand.

The ratio of what you do and do not understand will gradually change. I'm sure that you will experience this feeling in no time!

Step 2 - Step 1 was all about building the foundation in the Language. Your brain is learning to exist in this new Language. Remember, you are still a baby in this Language, so approach the Language in that way, take small baby steps. Don't be too disheartened if you don't understand something. This is natural and to be expected when learning a new language. In Step 2, we are actually "learning" the Language. Once you begin immersing yourself in the Language, you will notice a re-occurrence of words and phrases, which will trigger your memory. It would help if you were dying to find out the meaning of those continuously repetitive words and phrases that you have heard at this stage. In this phase, I recommend you to go back to the English translation and find the meaning of those words. I also recommend you go to the Arabic dictionary, as that will also allow you to search for the plural form of the noun or conjugate the verb further.

The critical point to remember from step 2 is that everything we have learned has emerged from the stories. It is recommended that you wait until you want to learn something, and then you look it up. The wisdom behind this is that everything we then learn becomes powerful. As we are ready for it, our brains are engaged. You will find that your natural curiosity will guide you towards effectively learning the vocabulary and remembering it well. The story always comes first!

Step 3 - in the third and last step, we focus on activating what we have learned by using the Language and putting it into practice. If you are coming from my previous book, "Arabic made easy: 100 Verbs in context", you will know how much I stressed this very topic. Until now, everything is happening inside of your head; we have built up the reservoir of knowledge. We have read, listened, learned. Now it's time to practice speaking. We take up the knowledge that we have built up from the stories and actively use it. The main idea here is to practice getting out what you have learned out of your mouth. There are no doubts that you will make plenty of mistakes, you will likely be laughed at, and you will struggle a lot at first, but this is the harsh reality of learning any language! What I would recommend you to do is:

- Try to find a person who is relatively fluent in Arabic and start engaging in conversation with them. Speak about the stories you have just learned from this book.

- If available, speak with a qualified Arabic teacher who can correct and help you work on your pronunciation.

- You will realize when you start speaking to others that you have now managed to internalize the grammar naturally and get it mostly correct, simply through reading, listening, and learning the stories repetitively. However, there will be plenty of things that you will not get right just yet, and that will come when you further progress into the Language and begin studying the books dedicated to grammar and morphology.

This three-stage process is a continuous cycle; you should continuously do it and make it a new habit of your life. One thing to note is that 80% of your time should be spent in the immersion phase (stage 1), continuously reading, listening and emerging yourself in the Language. You will realize that as your level progresses, you will find yourself reading more comprehensive texts. You may even reach a stage where you can move away from stories and focused on texts in your area of interest. For this to work effectively, I highly recommend you to follow along with the audiobook.

If you are coming from my previous book, Arabic made easy. You will know the importance of context and learning words in context. This now is a great opportunity for you to focus on the context in which the words are used. Please pay close attention to how certain verbs are used, what prepositions come before or after them. Don't focus too much on the grammar of the words, the ending of the word. Rather focus on how they are used in certain contexts. You will see certain words repeating themselves, and I have full confidence that you will be able to grasp the context in which those words are used. Listen attentively and keep on repeating the audio if you need to.

Note - In the Arabic language, we start from the right to the left, as opposed to the English language, where we read from left to right.

Note - Some words you will come across have a double silent vowel. Note that this is not correct and shouldn't be done when you are writing. The only reason I did it was so that the absolute beginner could follow along and manage to read the book. Please note that you can only have one silent vowel on a noun/verb.

Chapter 3: 50 Stories for beginners

الْقِصَّةُ الْأُولَى

قِصَّةُ حَمْزَةَ وَسَالِمِي

شَعَرَ حَمْزَةُ وَصَدِيقُهُ سَالِمِي بِالتَّعَبِ بَعْدَ يَوْمٍ طَوِيلٍ فِي الْمَدْرَسَةِ فَقَدْ كَانَ لَدَيْهِمْ بَعْضُ الْخُطَطِ فِي الْمَسَاءِ، وَلَكِنَّهُمْ لَمْ يَكُونُوا عَلَى يَقِينٍ مِمَّا إِذَا كَانُوا قَدْ يَتَقَدَّمُونَ فِي هَذِهِ الْخُطَطِ بِسَبَبِ مَدَى سُخْطِهِمْ .وَعِنْدَمَا وَصَلَ وَقْتُ الْمَسَاءِ، قَرَّرُوا إِلْغَاءَ خُطَطِهِمْ وَتَنَاوَلُوا الطَّعَامَ بَدَلاً مِنْ ذَلِكَ فِي مَطْعَمٍ مَعَ عَائِلَاتِهِمْ .وَلَقَدْ تَقَدَّمَ سَلْمَانُ شَقِيقُ حَمْزَةَ بِطَلَبِهِ عَلَى قَائِمَةِ الطَّعَامِ .طَلَبَ شَرَائِحَ اللَّحْمِ وَالْبُرْجَرِ وَبَطَاطًا مَقْلِيَّةً .فَضَّلَ سَلْمَانُ اللَّحْمَ الْبَقَرِيَّ عَلَى شَرَائِحِ اللَّحْمِ. كَانَ سَالِمِي نَبَاتِيًّا، لِذَا كَانَتْ قَائِمَةَ الطَّعَامِ فِي حَدٍّ أَدْنَى بِالنِّسْبَةِ لَهُ. بَعْدَ تَنَاوُلِ الْعَشَاءِ ، أَخَذَتْ الْعَائِلَةُ سَيَّارَةَ أُجْرَةً إِلَى الْمَنْزِلِ

Story 1

The story of Hamza and Salmi

Hamza and his friend Salmi both felt tired after a long day in school. They had some plans for the evening, but they weren't sure if they would go ahead with those plans because of how tired they were. When the evening time arrived, they decided to cancel their plans and instead eat at a restaurant with their family. Hamza's brother Salman made his order on the menu. He ordered a steak, burger and chips. Salman preferred beef to steak. Salmi was a vegan, so the menu was minimal for him. After eating their dinner, the family took a taxi home.

الْقِصَّةُ الثَّانِيَةُ

النَّمِرُ الْجَائِعُ

كَانَ هُنَاكَ نَمِرٌ فِي الْغَابَةِ .يَتَضَوَّرُ جُوعاً ، لِذَا كَانَ يَأْكُلُ أَيَّ حَيَوَانٍ حَوْلَهُ .وَكَانَ النَّمِرُ يَصْطَادُ أَرْنَبَ ثُمَّ أَكَلَهُ، رَغْمَ أَنَّهُ وَجَدَ أَنَّهُ لَمْ يَسْعِدْهُ وَرَغَبَاتُهُ. وَعِنْدَمَا سَمِعَتْ الْحَيَوَانَاتُ لْأُخْرَى عَنْ اِصْطِيَادِ النَّمِرِ لِلْاغْذِيَّةِ لَمْ يَكُنْ لَدَيْهِمْ خِيَارٌ آخَرُ سِوَى الْفِرَارِ مَدَى حَيَاتِهِمْ. اِجْتَمَعَتْ كُلُّ الْحَيَوَانَاتِ بِهُدُوءٍ مَعًا وَخَطَّطُوا لِلْخُرُوجِ مِنْ الْغَابَةِ .وَلَكِنْ بَعْدَ خُرُوجِهِمْ تَعَثَّرُوا لِلْأَسَفِ عَبْرَ النَّمِرِ وَصَرَخُوا فِيمَا بَيْنَهُمْ "إِهْرَبُوا

Story 2

The Hungry Tiger

There was a tiger in the forest. He was starving, so he ate any animal around him. The tiger hunted down a rabbit and ate him, though he found that it didn't satisfy him and his desires. When the other animals heard about the tiger's hunt for food, they became petrified; they had no other option but to flee for their life. All the animals quietly met together and planned their way out of the forest. Upon their exit, though, they, unfortunately, stumbled across the tiger. "Run!" they screamed amongst each other.

الْقِصَّةُ الثَّالِثَةُ

قَاتِلُ الْمُسَلْسَلِ

كَانَتْ صِفَارَاتُ الْإِنْذَارِ فِي جَمِيعِ أَنْحَاءِ الْمَدِينَةِ .لَقَدْ نَظَرْنَا إِلَى بَعْضِنَا الْبَعْضَ فِي حَالَةٍ مِنْ الِارْتِبَاكِ، وَلَمْ نَعْرِفْ مَا يَجْرِي وَلِمَاذَا كَانَتْ الْإِنْذَارَاتُ تَنْطَفِئُ .وَسُرْعَانَ مَا اِكْتَشَفْنَا أَنَّ الشُّرْطَةَ كَانَتْ تُلَاحِقُ سَفَّاحً .لَقَدْ أَصْبَحْنَا خَائِفِينَ، لِذَا قَرَّرْنَا الْبَقَاءَ فِي مَقْهًى فَارِغٍ .بَقِينَا هُنَاكَ حَتَّى تَوَقَّفَتْ صِفَارَاتُ الْإِنْذَارِ .وَبَعْدَ سَاعَةٍ اِنْتَقَلْنَا إِلَى الشَّارِعِ الرَّئِيسِيِّ، وَأَوْقَفَتْ الشُّرْطَةُ الْقَاتِلَ الْمُتَسَلْسِلَ! وَأَخِيراً أَصْبَحَ عَامَّةً النَّاسِ فِي حَالَةٍ مِنْ الرَّاحَةِ، مَعَ الْعِلْمِ بِأَنَّ الْقَاتِلَ لَنْ يُودِيَ بِحَيَاتِهِ إِلَى الْمَزِيدِ مِنْ الْأَرْوَاحِ .وَبَعْدَ ذَلِكَ بِأُسْبُوعَيْنِ، حُكِمَ عَلَيْهِ بِالسَّجْنِ مَدَى الْحَيَاةِ.

Story 3

The Serial Killer

There were sirens all around the city. We looked at each other in a state of confusion, not knowing what is going on and why the alarms were going off. We soon found out that the police were chasing a serial killer. We became terrified, so we decided to stay in an empty coffee shop. We stayed there until the sirens stopped. After an hour, we moved onto the main street, and the police had stopped the serial killer! The public was finally at ease, knowing that the killer would not be taking any more lives. Two weeks later, he was sentenced to life in prison.

الْقِصَّةُ الرَّابِعَةُ

أَنْطونِي وَخُطَّتَهُ

كَانَ وَالِدُ أَنْطونِي قَدْ تُوُفِّيَ فِي الْأَسْبُوعِ الْمَاضِي، فَتَرَكَهُ لِأُمِّهِ الْمُعَوَّقَةِ الَّتِي لَا تَسْتَطِيعُ أَنْ تَعْمَلَ. الْحَيَاةُ كَانَتْ صَعْبَةً لِأَنْتُونِي هَذَا الْإِسْبُوعِ وَقَدْ تَلَقَّى الْكَثِيرُ مِنْ التَّبَرُّعَاتِ مِنْ أَصْدِقَائِهِ وَعَائِلَتِهِ، وَلَكِنَّهُ يَعْلَمُ أَنَّهُ بِمُجَرَّدِ نَفَادِ الْأَمْوَالِ، سَيَكُونُ عَلَيْهِ أَنْ يُوَفِّرَ لِأُمِّهِ الْمُنْفَرِدَةِ، الَّتِي يَعْرِفُ أَنَّهَا سَتَكُونُ صَعْبَةً، لِأَنَّهُ مَا زَالَ مُرَاهِقاً، وَمِنْ الصَّعْبِ بِالنِّسْبَةِ لَهُ أَنْ يَجِدَ وَظِيفَةً فِي سِنِّهِ .لَدَى أَنْطونِي خُطَّةً .يُخَطِّطُ لِبَيْعِ الْوُرُودِ فِي الشَّارِعِ الْعَالِي لِتَوْفِيرِ وَالِدَتِهِ .إِذَا ذَهَبَ كُلُّ شَيْءٍ إِلَى الْخُطَّةِ ، إِنَّهُ سَيَكُونُ عَلَى مَا يُرَامُ

Story 4

Anthony and his plan

Anthony's father died last week, leaving him with his disabled mother, who cannot work. Life has been hard for Anthony this week. He has received a lot of donations from his friends and family, but he knows that once the money runs out, he will have to provide for his single mother, which he knows will be difficult, as he is still a teenager, and it is tough for him to find a job at his age. Anthony has a plan. He plans to sell roses in the high street to provide for his mother. If everything goes to plan, he should be fine.

الْقِصَّةُ الْخَامِسَةُ

غَابْرِيِيلْ وَجَدَتُهُ

كَانَ غَابْرِيِيلْ عَلَى عَلَاقَةٍ وَثِيقَةٍ لِلْغَايَةِ بِجِدَّتِهِ. رَبَّتَهُ عِنْدَمَا كَانَ قَلِيلًا بَيْنَ إِخْوَتِهِ. بَعْدَ ظُهْرِ يَوْمِ الْجُمْعَةِ، تَلَقَّى غَابْرِيِيلْ مُكَالَمَةً هَاتِفِيَّةً مِنْ وَالِدِهِ يُخْبِرُهُ بِأَنَّ جَدَّتَهُ مَرِيضَةٌ فِي الْمُسْتَشْفَى .بَدَأَ غَابْرِيِيلْ فِي الْهَلَعِ إِلَى أَنْ هَدَأَهُ وَالِدُهُ مِنْ مَنْصِبِهِ .فَقَدْ شَعَرَ غَابْرِيِيلْ بِكُلِّ سُهُولَةٍ حِينَ قَالَ" :إِنَّهُ مَرَضٌ خَفِيفٌ"، فَهُوَ يَعْلَمُ أَنَّ جَدَّتَهُ سَوْفَ تَكُونُ عَلَى مَا يَرَامُ .وَبِمُجَرَّدِ أَنْ قَطَعَ الْهَاتِفُ، سَارَعَ إِلَى الْمُسْتَشْفَى لِرُؤْيَةِ جَدَّتِهِ.

Story 5

Gabriel and his grandmother

Gabriel had a very close relationship with his grandmother. She raised him when he was little, among his brothers. On Friday afternoon, Gabriel received a phone call from his father telling him that his grandmother is ill in hospital. Gabriel began panicking until his father calmed him down. "It's only a mild illness, the doctor said" Gabriel felt at ease knowing that his grandmother would be fine. As soon as he cut the phone, he rushed to the hospital to see his grandmother.

الْقِصَّةُ السَّادِسَةُ

الْجِبَالِ

.كَانَتْ آمِي تَعِيشُ مَعَ عَائِلَتِهَا فِي مَنْزِلٍ كَبِيرٍ بِالْقُرْبِ مِنْ الْجِبَالِ
.عَاشَتْ فِي مَكَانٍ هَادِئٍ مُحَاطٍ بِالْأَشْجَارِ وَأَصْوَاتِ الْكِلَابِ الَّتِي تَنْبَحُ
.فِي أَحَدِ الْأَيَّامِ أَثْنَاءَ اللَّيْلِ، سَمِعْت آمِي خُطُوَاتٍ تَقْتَرِبُ مِنْ بَابِهَا
.وَأَصْبَحَتْ خَائِفَةً وَأَخْبَرَتْ عَائِلَتَهَا عَلَى الْفَوْرِ بِمَا سَمِعْتُهُ لِلتَّوِّ
.غَادَرَ الْأَبُ الْمَنْزِلَ بِسِلَاحٍ مُسْتَعِدّ لِلدِّفَاعِ عَنْ عَائِلَتِهِ حَتّى أَدْرَكَ
.أَنَّهُ كَانَ رَجُلَ التَّسْلِيمِ

Story 6

The mountains

Amy was living with her family in a big house near the mountains. She lived in a quiet place that was surrounded by trees and the sounds of dogs growling. One day during the nighttime, Amy heard footsteps approaching her door. She became terrified and immediately told her family what she just heard. The father left the house with a weapon, ready to defend his family until he realized that it was the delivery man.

الْقِصَّةُ السَّابِعَةُ

سَعْدٌ وَسُلُوكُهُ

سَعْدٌ طَالِبٌ فِي الْمَدْرَسَةِ الِابْتِدَائِيَّةِ .كَانَ دَائِماً صَبِيًّاً شَقِيًّاً .وَهُوَ يَضَعُ نَفْسَهُ دَوْماً فِي الْمَتَاعِبِ .فَهُوَ كَثِيراً مَا يَرْسَمُ عَلَى اللَّوْحَةِ، وَيَأْكُلُ طَعَامَ صَدِيقِهِ مِنْ دُونِ إِذْنِهِ، وَيَتَحَدَّثُ مَعَ زُمَلَائِهِ فِي الصَّفِّ بَيْنَمَا يُقَدِّمُ الْمُعَلِّمُ الدَّرْسَ .وَفِي الدَّاخِلِ، يُشَكِّلُ إِدَارَتُهُ تَحَدِّيًا كَبِيرًا .فَأَبَوَيْهِ يَعْمَلُونَ دَائِمًا، وَ ذَلِكَ الْأَمْرُ الَّذِي يُتْرَكُ لَهُ هُوَ وَأُخْتُهُ فِي الْبَيْتِ وَحْدَهُ .فَهُوَ يُقَاتِلُ دَائِمًا مَعَ أُخْتِهِ وَيَأْخُذُ أَمْتِعَتَهَا وَيَصْرُخُ عَلَيْهَا .ذَاتَ يَوْمٍ، اِشْتَكَتْ أُخْتُهُ لِوَالِدَيْهَا مِنْ الْكَيْفِيَّةِ الَّتِي تَعَامَلَ بِهَا سَعْدٌ مَعَهَا، فَقَرَّرَ وَالِدُهَا مُعَاقَبَةَ سَعْدٍ، وَلَمْ يَكُنْ مَسْمُوحاً لَهُ عَلَى جِهَازِ الْبِلَايْ سِتِيشَنْ لِمُدَّةِ أُسْبُوعَيْنِ! وَحِينَ اِكْتَشَفَ سَعْدٌ أَصْبَحَ نَادِمًا لِلْغَايَةِ، إِلَّا أَنَّهُ فَاتَ الْأَوَانُ

Story 7

Sa’ad and his behavior

Sa’ad is a student in primary school. He has always been a naughty boy. He always gets himself into trouble. He frequently draws on the noticeboard, eats his friend’s food without their permission, and talks to his classmates while the teacher delivers the lesson. At home, he is challenging to manage. His parents are always working, which leaves him and his sister at home alone. He always fights with his sister, takes her belongings and shouts at her. One day, his sister complained to her parents about how Sa’ad was treating her, her father decided to punish Sa’ad. he wasn’t allowed on the PlayStation for two weeks! When Sa’ad found out, he became very regretful, but it was too late!

الْقِصَّةُ الثَّامِنَةُ

مُسْتَقْبَلِي

لَقَدْ أَجْرَيْتُ مُحَادَثَةٌ صَادِقَةٌ مَعَ عَائِلَتِي حَوْلَ مُسْتَقْبَلِي .كَانَتْ أُمِّي تُرِيدُ دَوْماً أَنْ أَذْهَبَ إِلَى الْجَامِعَةِ وَأَنْ أَصْبَحَ طَبِيباً، وَلَكِنَّنِي لَا أُرِيدُ أَنْ أَفْعَلَ ذَلِكَ قَطُّ .لَمْ أَكُنْ رَاغِباً قَطُّ فِي الْمُرُورِ عَبْرَ مَسَارِ الْجَامِعَةِ، وَلَكِنَّنِي لَمْ أَكُنْ أَعْلَمُ !كَيْفَ أُخْبِرَ أُمِّي .بِغَضِّ النَّظَرِ عَنْ كَيْفِيَّةِ شَرْحِي لِخُطَّتِي، فَإِنَّهَا سَتَخْرُجُ فِي الْأُسْبُوعِ الْمَاضِي حَصَلْتُ عَلَى عَرْضٍ لِوَظِيفَةٍ رَائِعَةٍ فِي وَسَطِ لَنْدَنْ .لَقَدْ عَرَضْتُهَا .كَانَتْ مُتَشَكِّكَةً فِي الْبِدَايَةِ، وَلَكِنَّنِي شَرَحْتُ لَهَا خُطَّتِي الْمِهْنِيَّةَ وَكَيْفَ سَأُحَقِّقُ أَهْدَافِي .وَ بَعْدَ مَا فَعَلْتُ ذَلِكَ، شَعَرَتْ بِثِقَةٍ أَكْبَرَ وَأَخْبَرَتْنِي بِالْمَضِيِّ قُدُمًا فِي خُطَطِي.

Story 8

My Future

I had an honest conversation with my family about my future. My mother always wanted me to go to university and become a doctor, but I never really wanted to do that. I never really wanted to go through the university route, but I didn't know how to tell my mother. No matter how I would explain to her my plan, she would flip out! Last week I got an offer for a great job in central London. I showed her the offer. She was skeptical at first, but I explained my career plan and how I would achieve my goals. After I did that, she felt more confident and told me to go ahead with my plans.

الْقِصَّةُ التَّاسِعَةُ

سَفِينَتُنَا

لَقَدْ كَانَ يَوْماً عَاصِفاً مُمْطِراً عِنْدَمَا كُنَّا نَبْحَرُ فِي قَارِبِنَا .وَمِمَّا يُثِيرُ دَهْشَتَنَا أَنَّ هَذَا الْيَوْمَ كَانَ أَكْثَرَ هِرَابًا .لَمْ أَكُنْ أَعْتَقِدُ أَنَّنَا كُنَّا سَنَنْجُو مِنْ ذَلِكَ، فَقَدْ ظَنَنْتُ أَنَّنَا سَوْفَ نَصْطَدِمُ عَلَى شَاطِئِ جَزِيرَةٍ مَا .كُنَّا نُصَلِّي، لَمْ يَكُنْ لَدَيْنَا أَمَلٌ كَبِيرٌ .فَجْأَةً، مِنْ لَا مَكَانَ، رَأَيْنَا سَفِينَةً أُخْرَى كَانَتْ عَلَى بُعْدِ بِضْعِ مِئَاتٍ مِنْ الْأَمْتَارِ مِنَّا، وَصَرَخْنَا وَصَرَخْنَا نَحْوَ ذَلِكَ الِاتِّجَاهِ، لَقَدْ سَمِعُونَا لِحُسْنِ الْحَظِّ وَخَرَجُونَا إِلَى إِنْقَاذِنَا، وَكُنَّا مُمْتَنِّينَ لِلْغَايَةِ لِمُسَاعَدَتِهِمْ لِأَنَّنَا لَمْ نَظُنَّ أَنَّنَا سَنَصِلُ إِلَى الْجَانِبِ الْآخَرِ مِنْ الْبَحْرِ

Story 9

Our ship

it was a rainy windy day when we were sailing our boat. To our surprise, this day was extra windy. I didn't think we were going to make it, I thought we were going to crash on the shore of an island. We were praying, we had little hope. Suddenly, out of nowhere, we saw another ship that was a few hundred meters away from us, we screamed and screamed towards that direction, they luckily heard us and came to our rescue. we were very grateful for their help because we didn't think that we would make it to the other side of the sea.

الْقِصَّةُ الْعَاشِرَةُ

سَامْ وَحَدِيقَةُ الْحَيَوَانِ

تَوَجَّهَ سَامْ وَمَجْمُوعَةُ أَصْدِقَائِهِ إِلَى حَدِيقَةِ الْحَيَوَانِ فِي رِحْلَتِهِمْ الْمَدْرَسِيَّةِ، كَانَتْ هَذِهِ هِيَ الْمَرَّةَ الْأُولَى الَّتِي يَقْضُونَهَا فِي حَدِيقَةِ الْحَيَوَانِ وَعَلَى الرَّغْمِ مِنْ حَمَاسَتِهِمْ، إِلَّا أَنَّهُمْ كَانُوا مُتَوَتِّرِينَ بِنَفْسِ الْقَدْرِ إِزَاءَ الْحَيَوَانَاتِ. وَكَانَتْ هَذِهِ هِيَ الْمَرَّةَ الْأُولَى الَّتِي يَرَى فِيهَا سَامْ قِرْدٍ فِي الْحَيَاةِ الْحَقِيقِيَّةِ. أَخْبَرَهُمْ الْمُعَلِّمُونَ بِالْبَقَاءِ البَعِيْدِ عَنْ الْحَيَوَانَاتِ حِفَاظًا عَلَى سَلَامَتِهِمْ، وَلَكِنْ لَدَى سَامْ خُطَطٍ أُخْرَى. كَانَ هُنَاكَ شَيْءٌ عَنْ هَذَا الْقِرْدِ الَّذِي نُقِلَ سَامَ نَحْوَهُ. لَقَدْ اِنْدَهَشَ مِنْ قُدْرَتِهِ عَلَى الْقَفْزِ وَمَا كَانَ مُحِبًّاً وَرِعَايَتُهُ تُجَاهَ الْحَيَوَانَاتِ الْأُخْرَى. بَنَى سَامْ عَلَاقَةً رَائِعَةً مَعَ الْقِرْدِ. وَلَقَدْ فُوجِئَ الْمُعَلِّمُونَ لِأَنَّهُمْ لَمْ يَرَوْا أَيَّ شَيْءٍ مِنْ هَذَا الْقَبِيلِ مِنْ قَبْلُ.

Story 10

Sam and the Zoo

Sam and his group of friends headed to the Zoo for their school trip. It was their first time in the Zoo, and even though they were excited, they were equally nervous about the animals. It was the first time Sam saw a monkey in real life. The teachers told them to stay a distance away from the animals for their own safety, but Sam had other plans. There was something about this monkey that swayed Sam towards it. He was amazed by its jumping ability and how loving and caring it was towards the other animals. Sam built a great relationship with the monkey. The teachers were surprised as they hadn't seen anything like this before.

الْقِصَّةُ الْحَادِيَةَ عَشْرَةَ

يَوْمَ الِاخْتِبَارِ

،كَانَتْ شَارْلُوتْ تَشْعُرُ بِالتَّوَتُّرِ الشَّدِيدِ فِي يَوْمِ اِمْتِحَانِهَا .كَانَتْ طَالِبَةً ذَكِيَّةً وَلَكِنَّ الْخَوْفَ مِنْ الْفَشَلِ بَدَأَ يَزْحِفُ إِلَى رَأْسِهَا .كَانَتْ لَدَيْهَا فِرَاشَاتٌ عِنْدَ دُخُولِهَا قَاعَةَ الِاخْتِبَارِ، وَلَكِنَّهَا كَانَتْ تَعْلَمُ أَنَّهَا سَتَفْعَلُ جَيِّداً لِأَنَّهَا رَاجَعَتْ بِقُوَّةٍ لِلِامْتِحَانَاتِ .كَانَتْ هَذِهِ الِاخْتِبَارَاتُ حَيَوِيَّةً لِأَنَّهَا تُقَرِّرُ أَيْنَ تَدْرُسُ فِي الْعَامِ الْقَادِمِ. وَكَانَتْ لَدَيْهَا دَرَجَةٌ مُسْتَهْدَفَةٌ تَحْتَاجُ إِلَى تَحْقِيقِهَا لِلدِّرَاسَةِ فِي جَامِعَتِهَا الْمَرْغُوبَةِ. بَعْدَ الِاخْتِبَارِ، شَعَرَتْ بِالثِّقَةِ وَبِسُهُولَةٍ، وَلَمْ تَتَمَكَّنْ ،مِنْ انْتِظَارِ نَتَائِجِ الِاخْتِبَارِ. بَعْدَ أُسْبُوعَيْنِ تَقْرِيباً حَصَلَتْ عَلَى نَتَائِجِهَا وَلَمْ يَكُنْ بِوُسْعِهَا أَنْ تَكُونَ أَكْثَرَ سَعَادَةً إِزَاءَ تَقْرِيرِهَا

Story 11

Exam day

Charlotte was feeling very nervous on the day of her exams. She was an intelligent student, but the fear of failing started creeping into her head. She had butterflies upon her entry into the examination hall, but she knew that she would do well because she revised hard for the exams. These exams were vital as they would decide where she is studying in the next year. She had a target grade that she needed to achieve to study in her desired university. After the exam, she felt confident, at ease and couldn't wait for her exam results. About two weeks later, she received her results, and she couldn't be happier with her report!

الْقِصَّةُ الثَّانِيَةَ عَشْرَةَ

إِبْرَاهِيمُ وَالسَّمَكُ

.إِبْرَاهِيمُ صَيَّادٌ مَوْهُوبٌ؛ فَهُوَ اِصْطَادَ الْأَسْمَاكَ مُنْذُ كَانَ طِفْلاً صَغِيراً .لَقَدْ تَعَلَّمَ كُلَّ مَا يَعْرِفُهُ مِنْ وَالِدِهِ، الَّذِي كَانَ مَوْهُوبٌ جِدَّاً، وَكَذَلِكَ صَيَّادٌ مَعْرُوفٌ بَيْنَ أَفْرَادِ الْمُجْتَمَعِ .فِي الْأُسْبُوعِ الْمَاضِي، كَانَتْ هُنَاكَ مُنَافَسَةُ صَيْدٍ مَحَلِّيَّةٍ شَارَكَ فِيهَا إِبْرَاهِيمُ .وَكَانَ أَصْغَرَ عَدَدٍ هُنَاكَ وَلَكِنَّ هَذَا لَمْ يُوقِفُهُ عَنْ الْمُشَارَكَةِ .كَانَ مِنْ الْوَاضِحِ أَنَّ مُنَافِسِيهِ قَدْ قَلَّلُوا مِنْ شَأْنِ ذَلِكَ بِسَبَبِ سِنِّهِ .وَعَلَى نَحْوٍ يُثِيرُ دَهْشَتَهُمْ أَنَّهُ تَمَكَّنَ مِنْ التَّغَلُّبِ عَلَيْهِمْ جَمِيعاً وَالْفَوْزِ بِالْمُنَافَسَةِ .لَقَدْ أَصَابَتْهُمْ بِالصَّدْمَةِ وَالْحَرَجِ "لَابُدَّ أَنْ يَكُونَ مَحْظُوظًا "!صَرَخَ أَحَدُهُمْ .لَمْ يَكُنْ ذَلِكَ مَرْحَلَةَ إِبْرَاهِيمَ بَلْ لَقَدْ اِسْتَخْدَمَ الْكَرَاهِيَةَ لِكَيْ يَتَحَوَّلَ إِلَى صَيَّادٍ أَكْثَرَ مَوْهِبَةً

Story 12

Ibrahim and the fish

Ibrahim is a talented fisherman; he's been catching fishes since he was a small child. He learned everything that he knew from his father, who was very talented and also a known fisherman amongst the community. Last week, there was a local fishing competition that Ibrahim participated in. He was the youngest there, but that did not stop him from participating. It was clear that his competitors underestimated him because of his age. To their surprise, he managed to beat them all and win the competition. It left them shocked and embarrassed. "He must have been lucky!" screamed one of them. This did not phase Ibrahim; instead, he used the hate to become an even more talented fisherman.

الْقِصَّةُ الثَّالِثَةَ عَشْرَةَ

حَفْلَاتُ الْغِنَاءِ الْخَاصَّةُ بِي

كَانَتْ اللَيْلَةَ الَتِي سَبَقَتْ حَفْلَ غِنَائِي الْمَدْرَسِّي الْمُوسِيقِيَّةَ .كُنْتُ مُتَوَتِّراً جِدَّاً حَيْثُ أَنَّنِي لَمْ أَتَعَرَّضْ أَمَامَ حَشْدٍ كَبِيرٍ مِثْلَ هَذَا مِنْ قَبْلُ .كِدْتُ أَشْعُرُ كَأنَنِي عَلَىَ وَشْكِ الإِغْمَاءِ .لَمْ أَتَمَكَّنْ مِنْ تَحَمُّلِ الضَّغْطِ لِفَتْرَةٍ أَطْوَلَ رَأَتْنِي أُمِّي فِي هَذِهِ الْحَالَةِ، وَلَطَفَتْنِي عَلَى الْفَوْرِ" .الشُّعُورُ بِالتَّوَتُّرِ قَبْلَ. أَنْ يَكُونَ الْأَدَاءُ طَبِيعِيًّا، يَشْعُرُ أَفْضَلُ الْمُؤَدِّيِينَ بِالْأَعْصَابِ، وَلَكِنْ .كَيْفَ تَصَدَّتَ لِأَعْصَابِكَ عَلَى مَرْحَلَةٍ مُهِمَّةٍ"، نَصِيحَةُ أُمِّي عَلَقَتْ مَعِي .فِي يَوْمِ الْأَدَاءِ، تَمَكَّنْتُ مِنْ حَجْبِ أَعْصَابِي، وَ غَنَنْتُ بِصَوْتٍ جَمِيلٍ

Story 13

My singing concerts

It was the night before my school singing concert. I was very nervous as I hadn't performed Infront of a large crowd like this before. I almost felt like I was going to pass out. I couldn't bear the pressure for much longer. My mother saw me in this state, and she immediately comforted me. "Feeling nervous before a performance is normal, the best of performers feel nerves, but it's how you combat your nerves on stage that matters," my mother's advice stuck with me. On the performance day, I managed to withhold my nerves, and I sang with a beautiful voice.

الْقِصَّةُ الرَّابِعَةَ عَشْرَةَ

فَيْرُوسُ التَّاجِي

لَقَدْ أَثَّرَ وَبَاءُ فَيْرُوسِ التَّاجِي عَلَى حَيَاتِي وَمَا أَقُومُ بِهِ يَوْمِيًّا .قَبْلَ ظُهُورِ الْفَيْرُوسِ، كَانَ كُلُّ شَيْءٍ جَيِّداً، وَكَانَتْ وَظِيفَتِي آمِنَةً، وَكُنْتُ فِي صِحَّةٍ جَيِّدَةٍ .فَجْأَةً، فَقَدْتُ وَظِيفَتِي، أَتَعَافَى مِنْ الْفَيْرُوسِ، وَأَنَا عَاطِلٌ حَالِيًّا عَنْ الْعَمَلِ. عَلَى الرَّغْمِ مِنْ صُعُوبَةِ الْأَمْرِ بِالنِّسْبَةِ لِي فِي الْوَقْتِ الْحَالِيِّ، إِلَّا أَنَّنِي أَعْلَمُ أَنَّ الصَّبْرَ فَضِيلَةٌ مُهِمَّةٌ يَجِبُ أَنْ نَتَحَلَّى بِهَا، خَاصَّةً فِي أَوْقَاتِ الصُّعُوبَاتِ. أَنَا أَعْلَمُ أَنَّ رَبِّي لَنْ يَتْرُكَنِي وَسَيُبَارِكُنِي بِكُلِّ مَا أُصَلِّي مِنْ أَجْلِهِ إِنْ شَاءَ اللَّهُ

Story 14

Coronavirus

The coronavirus pandemic has affected my life and what I do on a day-to-day basis. Before the virus, everything was good, my job was secure, and I was in good health. All of a sudden, I've lost my job, I'm recovering from the virus, and I am currently unemployed. Even though it's difficult for me right now, I know that patience is an important virtue to have, especially in times of difficulty. I know that my lord will not forsake me and will bless me with everything that I pray for, God willing.

الْقِصَّةُ الْخَامِسَةُ عَشْرَةَ

هَاتِفِي الْمَفْقُودِ

فِي اللَّيْلَةِ الْمَاضِيَةِ ذَهَبْتُ إِلَى حَفْلِ عِيدِ مِيلَادِ صَدِيقِي فِي قَاعَةٍ صَغِيرَةٍ اِسْتَأْجَرَهَا. وَلَقَدْ اِسْتَمْتَعْتُ بِهِ حَقًّا، وَكَانَتْ نِسْبَةُ الْمُشَارَكَةِ كَبِيرَةً. لَقَدْ !حَظِّيْنَا بِوَقْتٍ رَائِعٍ إِلَى أَنْ أَدْرَكْتُ أَنَّ جَيْبِي كَانَ فَارِغاً ، وَاخْتَفَى هَاتِفِي بَدَأَ قَلْبِي يَتَسَابَقُ بِسُرْعَةٍ. أَدْرَكْتُ أَنَّنِي لَا أَسْتَطِيعُ أَنْ أَفْقِدَ هَذَا الْهَاتِف. فَقَدْ كَانَ الْهَاتِفُ الَّذِي اِشْتَرَاهُ وَالِدِي فِي عِيدِ مِيلَادِي الْخَامِسَ عَشَرَ .وَكَانَ وَالِدَيَّ لِيَنْقَلِبُوا لَوْ عَلِمُوا عَنْ هَاتِفِي الْمَفْقُودِ .كُنْتُ عَلَى اِسْتِعْدَادٍ لِالْعُثُورِ .عَلَيْهَا .وَلَمْ أَكُنْ عَلَى اِسْتِعْدَادٍ لِلْعَوْدَةِ إِلَى الدَّارِ خَالِياً مِنْ الْوِفَاضِ .لِحُسْنِ الْحَظِّ بِالنِّسْبَةِ لِي، قَامَ شَخْصٌ غَرِيبٌ بِالِاصْطِدَامِ عَلَى الْبَابِ وَأَعَادَنِي هَاتِفِي الْمَحْمُولِ بِأَمَانٍ، تَبَيَّنَ أَنَّهُ خَرَجَ مِنْ جَيْبِي فِي الطَّرِيقِ إِلَى الْحَفْلِ .كُنْتُ شَاكِرًا جِدًّا!

Story 15

My missing phone

Last night I went to my friend's birthday party in a small hall that he rented, I really enjoyed it, and the turnout was great. We had a great time until I realized that my pockets were empty, my phone disappeared! My heart began racing rapidly. I knew that I couldn't afford to lose this phone, it was the phone my father bought me for my 15th birthday. My parents would have flipped out if they knew of my missing phone. I was prepared to find it. I wasn't willing to go home empty-handed. Luckily for me, a stranger knocked on the door and returned me my mobile phone safely, it turned out that it slipped out of my pocket on the way to the party. I was so grateful!

الْقِصَّةُ السَّادِسَةَ عَشْرَ

الشَّاطِئُ

كُنْتُ أَرْغَبُ دَائِماً فِي الذَّهَابِ إِلَى الشَّاطِئِ كَطِفْلٍ .وَكَانَ أَسْعَدَ أَيَّامِ أَيِّ طِفْلٍ .اليَوْمَ كَانَ أَخِيْراً ذَلِكَ اليَوْم .لَقَدْ شَقَقْتُ طَرِيقِي إِلَى الشَّاطِئِ مَعَ أَفْضَلِ أَصْدِقَائِي رُونَا وَ عِصَامٍ .كَانَ يَوْماً مُشَمَّساً جَمِيلاً، بَيْنَمَا كُنَّا نَلْعَبُ عَلَى الرِّمَالِ وَنُشَاهِدُ الطَّائِرَاتِ الْوَرَقِيَّةَ تُطِيرُ بَعِيداً، كَانَ لَدَيْنَا الْكَثِيرُ مِنْ الْمَرَحِ !بَعْدَ فَتْرَةٍ، مَلَلْنَا مِنَ الطَّائِرَاتِ الْوَرَقِيَّةِ .أَرَدْنَا السِّبَاحَةَ فِي حَوْضِ. الْبَحْرِ ، وَلَكِنْ قِيلَ لَنَا أَنَّ هُنَاكَ أَسْمَاكَ الْقِرْشِ فِي الْبَحْرِ .لَقَدْ سَلَكْنَا قَفْزَةً هَائِلَةً فِي الْإِيمَانِ وَبَدَأْنَا فِي السِّبَاحَةِ .فِي الْبِدَايَةِ، كَانَ لَا بَأْسَ بِهِ، وَلَكِنْ بَعْدَ ذَلِكَ سَمِعْنَا ضَوْضَاءَ غَرِيبَةً مِنْ قَاعِ الْبَحْرِ، كَانَ يَقْتَرِبُ مِنَّا بِسُرْعَةٍ، كَانَتْ أَسْمَاكُ الْقِرْشِ !وَمِنْ حُسْنِ الْحَظِّ أَنَّنَا لَمْ نَسْبَح بَعِيدًا، لِذَا فَقَدَ عُدْنَا عَلَى الْفَوْرِ.

Story 16

The Beach

I have always wanted to go to the beach as a child. It was any child's happiest day. Today was finally that day. I made my way to the beach with my best friends Rona and Esam. It was a beautiful sunny day, as we played on the sand watching our kites fly away, we had so much fun! After a while, we got bored of the kites. We wanted to swim in the sea, but we were told that there were sharks in the sea. We took a huge leap of faith and began swimming. At first, it was okay, but then we heard a weird noise from the bottom of the sea, it was approaching us at a quick pace, it was the sharks! Thankfully we didn’t swim too far away, so we immediately returned.

الْقِصَّةُ السَّابِعَةَ عَشْرَةَ

الطَّبِيبُ الَّذِي يُسَافِرُ

جَارِيْ طَبِيبٌ مُؤَهَّلٌ. فَهُوَ كَانَ يُسَافِرُ فِي مُخْتَلِفِ أَنْحَاءِ الْعَالَمِ طِيلَةَ الْعَامَيْنِ الْمَاضِيَيْنِ يُعَالِجُ أَمْرَاضَ النَّاسِ. إِنَّهُ بَطَلٌ حَقِيقِيٌّ فِي أَعْيُنِنَا. هُنَاكَ أَمْرٌ وَاحِدٌ أَتَسَاءَلُ عَنْهُ دوماً، أَلَا وَهُوَ لِمَاذَا يَخْتَارُ السَّفَرَ إِلَى دُوَلِ الْحَرْبِ الثَّالِثَةِ، بِمُرَتَّبٍ أَقَلَّ، وَبِلَا أُسْرَةٍ، وَظُرُوفٍ مَعِيشِيَّةٍ أَكْثَرَ صُعُوبَةً؟ لَقَدْ طَلَبْنَا مِنْ الطَّبِيبِ عِنْدَ عَوْدَتِهِ إِلَى الْبِلَادِ. وَكَانَ رَدُّهُ بَسِيطًا: "إِنَّ بِلَادَنَا عَامِرَةٌ بِالْأَطِبَّاءِ الْمُؤَهَّلِينَ الْقَادِرِينَ عَلَى خِدْمَةِ النَّاسِ، وَأُرِيدُ أَنْ أُحْدِقَ فَارِقاً فِي حَيَاةِ النَّاسِ الْأَقَلِّ حَظًّا، وَلَا يَتَعَلَّقُ الْأَمْرُ بِالْمَالِ بِالنِّسْبَةِ لِي"، وَهُوَ مَا فَهِمَهُ النَّاسُ الْآنَ وَاسْتَفَادُوا مِنْهُ دَرْساً عَظِيمًا.

Story 17

The travelling doctor

My neighbor is a qualified doctor. He has been traveling all over the world for the last two years, curing people's diseases. He is a true hero in our eyes. One thing that I always wonder about him is, why does he choose to travel to 3rd war countries, with a lower salary, no family, and more difficult living conditions? we asked the doctor upon his return to the country. His reply was simple, "Our country is filled with qualified doctors that can serve the people, I want to make a difference in people's lives who are less fortunate, it isn't about the money for me" the people now understood and took a great lesson from his reasoning.

الْقِصَّةُ الثَّامِنَةَ عَشْرَةَ

الْحَشَرَةُ

كَانَ هُنَاكَ خَنْفِسَاءُ فِي مَنْطِقَتِنَا. كَانَتْ تَمْشِي بِرَشَاقَةٍ وَتَتَبَاهَى لَوْنَهَا الْأَحْمَرُ وَالْأَسْوَدُ. الْخَنْفِسَاءُ تُمْكِنُ أَنْ تَرَى الْمَمْلَكَةَ التَّفْتِيش يَنْظُرُ إِلَيْهَا بِإِعْجَابٍ كَبِيرٍ ، وَمَعَ ذَلِكَ، الْخَنْفِسَاءُ أَخَذَتْ الْقَلِيلِ مِنْ الِانْتِبَاهِ. وَبَعْدَ خُطُوَاتٍ قَلِيلَةٍ ، سَمِعَتْ الْخَنْفِسَاءُ سِلْسِلَةً مِنْ أَصْوَاتِ الطَّنِينِ. الْخَنْفِسَاءُ عَرَفَتْ أَنَّهُ صَوْتُ نَحْلَةٍ ذَكَرٍ! " ابْتَعِدْ عَنِّي! صَرَخَتْ السَّيِّدَةُ. ضَحِكَ النَّحْلُ وَأَجَابَ: "أَنْتِ حَقًّا حَشَرَةٌ عَدِيمَةُ الْفَائِدَةِ" هَذَا تَرَكَ الْخَنْفِسَاءُ حَزِينَةً وَجَعَلَهَا تَبْكِي ، وَفِيْ وَقْتٍ لَاحِقٍ تَمَّ إِرْضَاؤُهَا مِنْ قِبَلِ أَصْدِقَائِهَا.

Story 18

The ladybug

There was a ladybug in our area. she was walking gracefully and flaunting her red and black color. The ladybug could see the inspect kingdom looking at her with great admiration, yet the ladybug took little notice. A few strides later and the ladybug heard a series of buzzing noises. The ladybug knew it was the sound of a male bee! "Get away from me! screamed the lady bug" the bee laughed and replied, "you really are a useless insect" this left the ladybug sad and made her cry, later she was comforted by her friends.

الْقِصَّةُ التَّاسِعَةُ عَشْرَةَ

أَحْلَامِي

أَتَذَكَّرُ عِنْدَمَا سُئِلْتُ عِنْدَمَا كُنْتُ طِفْلًا ، "مَاذَا تُرِيدُ أَنْ تَكُونَ عِنْدَمَا تَكْبُرُ". كَانَتْ إِجَابَتِي هِيَ نَفْسَهَا بِمَا أَنَّنِي أَسْتَطِيعُ أَنْ أَتَذَكَّرَ "أُرِيدُ أَنْ أَكُونَ لَاعِبَ كُرَةِ قَدَمٍ". كُرَةُ الْقَدَمِ كَانَتْ الرِّيَاضَةَ الْأَكْثَرَ شَعْبِيَّةً فِي بَلَدِنَا وَوَاحِدَةً مِنْ أَكْثَرِ الرِّيَاضَاتِ شَعْبِيَّةً فِي الْعَالَمِ. كُنْتُ أَعْرِفُ أَنَّهُ إِذَا كُنْتُ لِجَعْلِهِ كَلَاعِبِ كُرَةِ قَدَمٍ ، يَجِبُ أَنْ يَكُونَ الْآنَ ، وَقْتِي يَنْفُذُ ، وَالْمُنَافَسَةُ تَزْدَادُ قُوَّةً فَقَطْ كُلَّ عَامٍ. سَجَّلْتُ لِمُحَاكَمَةٍ لِنَادِي مُحْتَرِفٍ. الْمُحَاكَمَةَ الْأُسْبُوعَ الْقَادِمَ . وَآمُلُ أَنْ يَتِمَّ اخْتِيَارِي وَأُحَقِّقُ أَحْلَامِي

Story 19

My dreams

I remember being asked as a child, “what do you want to be when you grow up” my answer was the same since I can remember “I want to be a footballer!” many kids around the country also shared this same dream with me, football was the most popular sport in our country, and one of the most popular sports in the world. I knew that if I were to make it as a footballer, it would have to be now, my time is running out, and the competition is only getting stronger every year. I signed up for a trial for a professional club. The trial is next week, and I hope I get selected and achieve my dreams.

الْقِصَّةُ الْعِشْرِينَ

يَوْمَ التَّخَرُّجُ

الْأُسْبُوعُ الْقَادِمُ هُوَ أُسْبُوعُ تَخَرُّجِي ، الْأُسْبُوعَ الَّذِي كُنْتُ أَعْمَلُ مِنْ أَجْلِهِ عَلَى مَدَى السَّنَوَاتِ الْأَرْبَعِ الْمَاضِيَةِ. لَا أُصَدِّقُ مَدَى سُرْعَةِ مُرُورِ السِّنِينَ. بِالتَّأْكِيدِ سَأَفْتَقِدُ الْجَامِعَةَ. كَانَتْ ، بِلَا شَكٍّ ، أَفْضَلَ أَرْبَعِ سَنَوَاتٍ مِنْ حَيَاتِي. لَقَدْ جَعَلْتُ بَعْضَ مِنْ أَصْدِقَائِي الْمُقَرَّبِينَ خِلَالَ هَذِهِ السَّنَوَاتِ الْأَرْبَعِ. وَيَتَعَيَّنُ عَلَيَّ الْآنَ أَنْ أُعِدَّ نَفْسِي لِعَالَمِ الْعَمَلِ ،عَالَمٌ الَّذِي أَنَا قَلِقٌ حَوْلَ التَّدَخُّلِ فِيهِ ، أَنَا أَنْطِوَائِي ، وَأَنَا أُحِبُّ أَنْ أَبْقَى نَفْسِي لِنَفْسِي. آمَلُ أَنْ أَجِدَ دَوْرًا يُنَاسِبُ شَخْصِيَّتِي.

Story 20

Graduation day

Next week is my graduation week, the week that I have been working towards for the last four years. I can't believe how fast the years passed by. I will definitely miss university. It was, without a doubt, the best four years of my life. I have made some of my closest friends during these four years. I now have to prepare myself for the world of work, a world in which I am anxious about stepping in, I am an introvert, and I like to keep myself to myself. I hope I can find a role that suits my personality.

الْقِصَّةُ الْحَادِيَةُ وَالْعِشْرِينْ

الزَّنْجَبِيلُ

الطَّاهِي فِي مَدِينَتِنَا كَانَ الْأَفْضَلَ فِي صُنْعِ خُبْزِ الزَّنْجَبِيلِ. الْأُسْبُوعَ الْمَاضِيَ كَانَ لَدَيْهِ لَيْلَةٌ مَفْتُوحَةٌ حَيْثُ كَانَ يُعْطِي وَصْفَتَهُ السِّرِّيَّةَ مَجَّانًا حَضَرْتُ ، وَاسْتَمَعْتُ بِاهْتِمَامٍ. تَنَاوَلَ الطَّاهِي أَوَّلاً كَمِّيَّةً صَغِيرَةً مِنْ. الطَّحِينِ وَالْمَاءِ فَضْلاً عَنْ السُّكَرِ وَالزَّنْجَبِيلِ. ثُمَّ خَلَطَهُمْ وَأَضَافَ كَمِّيَّةً صَغِيرَةً مِنْ الْمَاءِ لِرَقِيقِ الْمَزِيجِ ، وَكَمِّيَّةً صَغِيرَةً مِنْ الطَّحِينِ لِتَسْخِينِهِ ، وَقَلِيلٌ مِنْ الْمِلْحِ وَالْخَمِيرَةِ. حَوَّلَ هَذَا إِلَى عَجِينَةٍ صَفْرَاءَ شَاحِبَةٍ. ثُمَّ وَضَعَهُ فِي الْفُرْنِ لِمُدَّةِ خَمْسَ عَشْرَةَ دَقِيقَةً. بَعْدَ الِانْتِهَاءِ مِنْ الزَّنْجَبِيلِ ، كَانَ كُلٌّ مِنَّا جُزْءٌ صَغِيرٌ لِمُحَاوَلَةٍ ، وَ نَجَاحٌ بَاهِرٍ! "نَحْنُ بِالتَّأْكِيدِ يَجِبُ أَنْ نُجَرِّبَ هَذَا فِي الْمَنْزِلِ" ، قَالَتْ أُمِّي.

Story 21

Gingerbread

The chef in our city was the best at making gingerbread. Last week he had an open night where he was giving away his secret recipe for free. I attended and listened attentively. The chef first took a small amount of flour and water, as well as sugar and ginger. He then mixed them and added a small amount of water to thin the mix, a small amount of flour to thicken it, and a little salt and yeast. He turned this into a pale-yellow dough. He then put it in the oven for fifteen minutes. After the gingerbread was finished, we each had a small portion to try, and wow! "We definitely have to try this at home," said my mother.

الْقِصَّةُ الثَّانِيَةُ وَالْعِشْرِيْنْ

مِقْيَاسُ الْوَزْنِ

فَاطِمَةُ وَإِزْهَامُ وَزَنَتَا أَنْفُسَهُمَا عَلَى مِقْيَاسِ الْوَزْنِ. كِلْتَاهُمَا كَانَ لَدَيْهِ هَدَفٌ لِفِقْدَانِ كِيلُوغْرَامَيْنِ. اِتَّضَحَ أَنَّ إِيزْهَامْ فَقَدَتْ ارْبَعَ كِيلُوغْرَامَاتٍ فِي الْمَجْمُوعِ ، فِي حِينِ أَنَّ فَاطِمَةَ لَمْ تَفْقِدْ أَيَّ وَزْنٍ عَلَى الْإِطْلَاقِ. فَاطِمَةُ أَصْبَحَتْ مُحْبِطَةً وَمُشَوَّشَةً. مَا الَّذِي جَعَلَكِ تَفْقِدِينَ هَذَا الْوَزْنَ ؟ أَجَابَتْ إِيزْهَامْ: "لَقَدْ كَانَ لَدَيَّ دُرُوسٌ خَاصَّةٌ فِي الِاسْتُودْيُو". أُصِيبَتْ فَاطِمَةُ بِخَيْبَةِ أَمَلٍ بِسَبَبِ رَدِّهَا عَلَيْهَا ، حَيْثُ عَرَفَتْ أَنَّهَا لَا تَسْتَطِيعُ تَحَمُّلَ تَكَالِيفِ الْحُصُولِ عَلَى مُدَرِّبٍ خَاصٍّ. رَأَتْ إِيزْهَامْ خَيْبَةَ الْأَمَلِ وَقَالَتْ: "لَا تَقْلَقِي، سَأُعْطِيكِ نِظَامِي الْغِذَائِيَّ الَّذِي سَمَحَ لِي بِفِقْدَانِ كُلِّ هَذَا الْوَزْنِ" هَذَا الْخِيَارُ كَانَ أَكْثَرَ تَكْلِفَةً لِفَاطِمَةَ. فَجْأَةً تَحَوَّلَتْ الدُّمُوعُ إِلَى اِبْتِسَامَاتٍ "حَانَ الْوَقْتُ لِلْوُصُولِ إِلَى الْعَمَلِ!" قَالَتْ فَاطِمَةُ:

Story 22

The weighing scale

Fatma and Irham weighed themselves on the weighing scale. They both had a goal to lose two kilograms. It turned out that Irham lost four kilograms in total, whilst Fatma didn't lose any weight at all. Fatma became frustrated and confused. "What caused you to lose this weight?" she said curiously. Irham replied, "I have been having private studio classes." Fatma was disappointed by her response, as she knew that she couldn't afford to have a private instructor. Irham saw the disappointment and said, "Don't worry, I will give you my diet that allowed me to lose all of this weight" that option was more affordable for Fatma, suddenly the tears turned into smiles "it's time to get to work!" said Fatma.

الْقِصَّةُ الثَّالِثَةُ وَالْعِشْرِينْ

مَاجِدٌ وَشَقَّتُهُ

مَاجِدٌ كَانَ يَبْحَثُ عَنْ شَقَّةٍ جَدِيدَةٍ لِلْأَسْبُوعَيْنِ الْمَاضِيَيْنِ. هَذَا لِأَنَّ حَالِيَّتَهُ صَغِيرَةٌ جِدّاً ، وَيَرْغَبُ بِإِيوَاءِ عَائِلَتِهِ. أَمْسِ مَاجِدٌ صَادَفَ إِعْلَانً لِشَقَّةٍ مَحَلِّيَّةٍ الَّتِي اِسْتَوْفَتْ مُتَطَلَّبَاتِهِ. كَانَتْ رَخِيصَةً ، وَاسِعَةً وَنَظِيفَةً. الشَّقَّةُ كَانَ لَدَيْهَا تِلْفَازٌ ، طَبَّاخٌ ، غَسَّالَةٌ. بِرَغْمِ ذَلِكَ الْأَثَاثُ قَدِيمٌ وَيَلْزَمُ اِسْتِبْدَالُهُ. وَكَانَ مَاجِدٌ مُحَادَثَةً طَوِيلَةً مَعَ زَوْجَتِهِ ، كَمَا كَانُوا يَعْرِفُونَ أَنَّ هَذَا سَيَكُونُ اِسْتِثْمَارً بَاهِظَ الثَّمَنَ. وَفِي النِّهَايَةِ ، قَرَّرُوا عَدَمَ شِرَاءِ الشَّقَّةِ وَوَاصَلُوا بَحْثَهُمْ.

Story 23

Majid and his flat

Majid has been searching for a new flat for the last two weeks. This is because his current one is too small, and he wishes to accommodate his family. Yesterday Majid came across an advertisement for a local flat that met his requirements. It was cheap, spacious, and clean. The flat had a TV, a cooker, a washing machine. However, the furniture was old and needed replacing. Majid had a long conversation with his wife, as they knew that this would be an expensive investment. In the end, they decided against buying the flat and continued their search.

الْقِصَّةُ الرَّابِعَةُ وَالْعِشْرِينْ

اِجْتِمَاعُ سَارَّةَ

سَارَّةُ لَدَيْهَا اِجْتِمَاعُ عَمَلٍ لَاحِقاً مَعَ سَمِيْرْ. يُخَطِّطُونَ لِلاجْتِمَاعِ فِي مَطْعَمٍ قَرِيبٍ مِنْ الْمَنْطِقَةِ. سَارَّةَ لَا تَعْرِفُهُ ، لَكِنَّ صَدِيقَتَهَا صَدِيقَةٌ لِ سَمِيْرَ. لِذَا سَأَلَتْ سَارَّةَ صَدِيقَهَا عَنْ سَمِيْرْ. أَرَادَتْ أَنْ تَعْرِفَ كُلَّ التَّفَاصِيلِ عَنْهُ أَرَادَتْ إِغْلَاقَ الصَّفْقَةِ لِشَرِكَتِهَا. عِنْدَ لِقَائِهِمَا ، رَحَّبَتْ سَارَّةُ بِ سَمِيْرَ بِابْتِسَامَةٍ كَرِيمَةٍ. "سَرَرْتُ بِلِقَائِكَ". رَدَّ سَمِيْرْ عَلَى التَّحِيَّاتِ وَبَدَأُوا مُنَاقَشَةَ الْعَمَلِ. وَبَعْدَ الِاجْتِمَاعِ ، تَلَقَّتْ سَارَّةُ رِسَالَةً نَصِّيَّةً مِنْ سَمِيْرَ يَقُولُ فِيهَا أَنَّهُ مُهْتَمٌّ بِالْعَمَلِ مَعَهَا. قَفَزَتْ سَارَّةُ صُعُودًا وَهُبُوطًا مِثْلَ طِفْلٍ صَغِيرٍ. لَقَدْ كَانَتْ سَعِيدَةً جِدًّاً

Story 24

Sarah's meeting

Sarah has a business meeting later on with Sameer. They plan to meet in a restaurant close by to the area. Sara doesn't know him, but her friend is good friends with Sameer. So, Sara asked her friend about Sameer. She wanted to know every little detail about him. She wanted to close the deal for her company. Upon their meeting, Sara greeted Sameer with a gracious smile. "It's nice to meet you!" she said. Sameer replied to the greetings, and they began discussing business. After the meeting, Sara received a text message from Sameer, saying that he was interested in working with her. Sara jumped up and down like a small child. She was so happy!

الْقِصَّةُ الْخَامِسَةُ وَالْعِشْرِينْ

مُصْطَفَى وَوَظِيفَتُهُ الْجَدِيدَة

.مُنْذُ وَبَاءِ فَيْرُوسِ كُرُونَا ، كَانَ مُصْطَفَى يَبْحَثُ عَنْ وَظِيفَةٍ جَدِيدَةٍ بِقُوَّةٍ .الْأُسْبُوعَ الْمَاضِي حَصَلَ عَلَى دَعْوَةٍ لِمُقَابَلَةٍ. كَانَ وَاثِقاً لِأَنَّهُ ظَنَّ أَنَّهُ. أَجْرَ الْمُقَابَلَةَ بِشَكْلٍ جَيِّدٍ. الْيَوْمَ تَلَقَّى مُكَالَمَةً مِنْ الشَّرِكَةِ. تَمَّ قَبُولُ مُصْطَفَى وَكَانَ يَبْدَأُ الْأُسْبُوعَ الْقَادِمَ! مُصْطَفَى الْآنَ يَعُدُّ نَفْسَهُ عَقْلِيًّا لِإِعْدَادَاتِ عَمَلِ الشَّرِكَاتِ. هَذِهِ كَانَتْ وَظِيفَتَهُ الْأُولَى خَارِجَ الْجَامِعَةِ. كَانَ مُعْتَادًا عَلَى الْفُصُولِ الدِّرَاسِيَّةِ ، الْمَقَالَاتِ ، وَالْبَقَاءِ حَتَّى وَقْتٍ مُتَأَخِّرٍ. حَيَاتُهُ كُلُّهَا كَانَتْ عَلَى وَشْكِ أَنْ تَنْقَلِبَ. هَذَا الْأُسْبُوعَ ، يُخَطِّطُ لِتَغْيِيرِ نَمَطِ نَوْمِهِ شِرَاءُ الْمَزِيدِ مِنْ الْمَلَابِسِ لِلْعَمَلِ وَبَدْءِ التَّوَاصُلِ مَعَ زُمَلَائِهِ !الْمُقَرَّبِينَ

Story 25

Mustafa and his new job

Ever since the coronavirus pandemic, Mustafa has been searching for a new job vigorously. Last week he got invited for an interview. He was confident because he thought he did the interview well. Today he received a call from the company. Mustafa was accepted, and he was starting next week! Mustafa is now mentally preparing himself for corporate work settings. This was his first job out of university. He was used to classrooms, essays, and staying up late. His whole life was about to be flipped. This week, he plans to change his sleeping pattern, buy some more clothes for work and start reaching out to his soon-to be colleagues!

الْقِصَّةُ السَّادِسَةُ وَالْعِشْرِينْ

الْعُطْلَةَ

هَذِهِ الْجُمْعَةُ سَتَكُونُ آخِرَ يَوْمٍ لَنَا فِي الْمَدْرَسَةِ حَتَّى عُطْلَةَ الصَّيْفِ لِمُدَّةِ سِتَّةِ أَسَابِيعَ. أَنَا بِصَرَاحَةٍ لَا أَسْتَطِيعُ إِنْتِظَارَ هَذِهِ الْعُطْلَةِ. هَذَا الْعَامَ كَانَ صَعْباً عَلَيّ. فَقَدَتُ وَالِدِي خِلَالَ الْفَتْرَةِ الْأُولَى بَيْنَمَا اضْطُرِرْتُ لِلاسْتِعْدَادِ لِلامْتِحَانَاتِ الفَتْرَةِ الثَانِيَةِ. لَوْ لَمْ يَكُنْ لِأَصْدِقَائِي الْمُسَاعِدِينَ لَا أَعْتَقِدُ أَنَّنِي كُنْتُ سَأَخْرُجُ هَذَا الْعَامَ. بِسَبَبِ كَمْ كَانَ أَصْدِقَائِي دَاعِمِينَ لِي، أُخَطِّطُ لِمُفَاجَئَتِهِمْ مَعَ عُطْلَةٍ فِي إِسْبَانْيَا. أَعْرِفُ بِأَنَّهُمْ أَرَادُوا دَائِماً لِلذِهَابِ إِلَى إِسْبَانْيَا. يُحِبُّونَ الْجَوَّ ، الْحَيَاةَ اللَّيْلِيَّةَ ، وَالطَّعَامَ. يَوْمَ الْجُمْعَةِ ، سَأُخْبِرُهُمْ بِخُطَّتِي. أَعْرِفُ بِأَنَّهُمْ سَيُحِبُّوْنَهَا.

Story 26

The Holidays

This Friday will be our last day in school until our six-week summer holiday break. I honestly can't wait for this holiday. This year has been very tough for me. I lost my father during the first term while I had to prepare for my exams for the 2nd term. Had it not been for my supportive friends, I don't think I would have made it out this year. Because of how supportive my friends have been of me; I plan to surprise them with a holiday in Spain. I know they have always wanted to go to Spain. They love the weather, the nightlife, and the food. On Friday, I will tell them of my plan, I know they will love it.

الْقِصَّةُ السَّابِعَةُ وَالْعِشْرِينْ

سَامْ وَسَيَّارَتُهُ

عَادَ سَامْ مِنْ عَمَلِهِ فِي سَيَّارَتِهِ الْجَدِيدَةِ. تَلَقَّى الْعَدِيدَ مِنْ الْمُجَامَلَاتِ وَالتَّهَانِي عَلَى سَيَّارَتِهِ الْجَدِيدَةِ. سَامْ كَانَ يَدْخَرُ لِهَذِهِ السَّيَّارَةَ خِلَالَ الْعَامَيْنِ الْمَاضِيَيْنِ. لَقَدْ كَانَ مُتَحَمِّسٌ لِلسَّيَّارَاتِ وَكَانَ يُحِبُّ صَوْتَ السَّيَّارَاتِ الرِّيَاضِيَّةِ. أَدْرَكَ وَالِدُ سَامْ أَنَّ سَامْ كَانَ سَائِقٌ مُتَهَوِّرٌ تَمَامًا ، لِذَا نَصَحَهُ ، "لَا يُمْكِنُكَ أَنْ تَقُودَ بِهَذِهِ السُّرْعَةِ عَلَى الطَّرِيقِ الرَّئِيسِيِّ سَامْ!" سَامْ لَمْ يَأْخُذْ بِنَصِيحَةِ وَالِدِهِ. وَبَعْدَ بِضْعِ لَيَالٍ ، تَوَرَّطَ فِي حَادِثِ سَيَّارَةٍ. لَيْسَ فَقَطْ لَمْ يُدَمِّرْ سَيَّارَتَهُ إِلَى قِطَعٍ ، وَلَكِنْ كَانَ عَلَيْهِ أَيْضًا لِدَفْعِ غَرَامَةٍ ضَخْمَةٍ عَلَى رَأْسِ ذَلِكَ.

Story 27

Sam and his car

Sam came back home from work in his brand-new car. He received many compliments and congratulations on his new car. Sam had been saving up for this car for the last two years. He was a massive car enthusiast and loved the sound of sports cars. Sam's dad realized that Sam was quite a reckless driver, so he advised him, "You can’t be driving that fast on the main road Sam! you will injure people if you continue to do this" Sam didn't take his father's advice. A few nights later, he was involved in a car accident. Not only did he destroy his car to bits, but he also had to pay a massive fine on top of that.

الْقِصَّةُ الثَّامِنَةُ وَالْعِشْرِينْ

أيمِي الرَّاقِصَة

أيمِي أَرَادَتْ أَنْ تَتَعَلَّمَ كَيْفَ تَرْقُصُ ، كَانَتْ تُحِبُّ الِاسْتِمَاعَ إِلَى الْمُوسِيقَى وَلَكِنْ حَانَ الْوَقْتُ الْآنَ لِتَعْلِيمِ كَيْفِيَّةِ الرَّقْصِ. أَخَذَتْ صَفَّهَا الرَّقْصَ الْأَوَّلَ أَمْسِ. أَمَرَتْ مُدَرِّبَةُ الرَّقْصِ لَهَا لِتَمْدِيدِ سَاقَيْهَا. حَاوَلَتْ عِدَّةَ مَرَّاتٍ لَكِنَّهَا لَمْ تَكُنْ قَادِرَةً عَلَى ذَلِكَ. قَالَتْ لَهَا الْمُدَرِّبَةُ: " عَلَيْكِ أَنْ تَتَمَدَّي يَوْمِيًّا حَتَّى تَتَمَكَّنِي مِنْ تَحْسِينِ مُرُوِّنَتِكِ". بَعْدَ الدَّرْسِ ، عَضَلَاتُهَا كَانَتْ مُؤْلِمَةً. لَمْ تَكُنْ مُعْتَادَةً عَلَى هَذَا الْمُسْتَوَى مِنْ الْكَثَافَةِ. "مَا زَالَ أَمَامَكِ طَرِيقٌ طَوِيلٌ قَبْلَ أَنْ تَبْدَئِي الرَّقْصَ بِنَجَاحٍ ، قَالَتْ الْمُعَلِّمَةُ".

Story 28

Amy the dancer

Amy wanted to learn how to dance, she loved listening to music, but it was now time to learn how to dance. She took her first dance class yesterday. The dance instructor instructed her to stretch out her legs. She tried multiple times, but she wasn't able to. The instructor told her, "You need to stretch on a daily basis so that you can improve your flexibility. After the lesson, her muscles were aching. She wasn't used to this level of intensity. "You still have a long way to go before you start dancing successfully, said the teacher."

الْقِصَّةُ التَّاسِعَةُ وَالْعِشْرِينْ

قِصَّةُ نَدَا

كَانَتْ نَدَا تُشْعُرُ بِالْمَلَلِ فِي الْمَنْزِلِ ، وَمَعَ وَظِيفَتِهَا الْحَالِيَّةِ ، فَعَلَتْ نَفْسُ الْأَشْيَاءِ بِشَكْلٍ مُتَكَرِّرٍ كُلَّ يَوْمٍ. أَرَادَتْ نَدَا لِمُمَارَسَةِ رِيَاضَةٍ جَدِيدَةٍ ، شَيْءٌ أَنَّهَا لَمْ تَفْعَلْ مِنْ قَبْلُ. فِي الْبِدَايَةِ ، حَاوَلَتْ نَدَا الطَّبْخَ ، لَكِنَّهَا لَمْ تَكُنْ أَفْضَلَ طَبَّاخَةٍ ، ثُمَّ حَاوَلَتْ السِّبَاحَةَ ، لَكِنَّهَا غَرِقَتْ تَقْرِيبًا. "أَنَا لَسْتُ جَيِّدَةً فِي أَيِّ شَيْءٍ أُمِّي ،" قَالَ نَدَا فِي نَبْرَةٍ مُخَيِّبَةٍ لِلْآمَالِ. أَجَابَتْ وَالِدَتُهَا ، "هَذَا لَيْسَ صَحِيحًا! لِمَاذَا لَا تُجَرِّبِينَ رُكُوبَ الدَّرَّاجَاتِ ؟ لَقَدْ كُنْتِ دَائِمًا تَرْكَبِينَ الدَّرَاجَةَ الْكَثِيرِ عِنْدَمَا كُنْتِ طِفْلَةً " ذَهَبَتْ نَدَا إِلَى الْأَمَامِ وَ حَاوَلَتْ رُكُوبَ الدَّرَّاجَاتِ لِأَوَّلِ مَرَّةٍ مُنْذُ فَتْرَةٍ طَوِيلَةٍ. اِسْتَمْتَعَتْ بِذَلِكَ وَخَطَّطَتْ لِبَدْءِ رُكُوبِ الدَّرَّاجَاتِ كُلَّ أُسْبُوعٍ

Story 29

The story of Nada

Nada was bored at home, and with her current job, she did the same things repetitively every day. Nada wanted to practise a new sport, something she has never done before. At first, Nada tried cooking, but she was not the best cook, then she tried swimming, but she nearly drowned. “I’m not good at anything mum,” said nada in a disappointing tone. Her mother replied, “That’s not true! why don’t you try cycling? you’ve always cycled a lot as a child” Nada went ahead and tried cycling for the first time in a long time. She enjoyed it and planned to start cycling every week.

الْقِصَّةُ الثَّلَاثِينَ

ابْنِي وَكَلْبِه

اِبْنِي لَمْ يَكُنْ لَدَيْهِ كَلْبٌ مِنْ قَبْلُ. إِنَّهُ يَطْلُبُ مِنِّي أَنْ أَحْصُلَ عَلَيْهِ مُنْذُ فَتْرَةٍ طَوِيلَةٍ. لَمْ أَكُنْ أَعْرِفُ مَا إِذَا كَانَ الْوَقْتُ الْمُنَاسِبُ بِالنِّسْبَةِ لَهُ لِلْحُصُولِ عَلَى كَلْبٍ ، لِذَلِكَ سَلَّيْتُ وَالِدَهُ. بَعْدَ عِدَّةِ سَاعَاتٍ مِنْ النِّقَاشِ ، اِتَّفَقْنَا عَلَى شِرَاءِ كَلْبِهِ الْأَوَّلِ. كَانَ جَرْوٌ صَغِيرٌ ، مَلِيءٌ بِالْحَيَاةِ ، اِبْنِي يُحِبُّ أَنْ يَلْعَبَ مَعَ هَذَا الْكَلْبِ وَيُخْرِجَهُ لِلْمَشْيِ كُلَّ صَبَاحٍ ، إِنَّهُ لَمْ يُفَوِّتْ صَبَاحً وَاحِدً حَتَّى الْآنَ! الْأُسْبُوعَ الْمَاضِي ، أَعْطَى الْجَرْوَ قِصَّةَ شَعْرٍ لَطِيفَةٍ وَاسْتِحْمَامٍ " أَنَا لَا أَسْتَطِيعُ الِانْتِظَارَ حَتَّى تَكْبَرَ " قَالَ الِابْنُ لِجَرْوِهِ.

Story 30

My son and his dog

My son has never had a dog before. He's been asking me to get him one for a long time now. I didn't know whether it was the right time for him to get a dog, so I consoled his father. After multiple hours of discussion, we agreed to buy him his first dog. It was a young puppy, full of life, my son loves to play with this dog and take it out for walks every morning, he hasn't missed a single morning so far! last week, he gave the puppy a nice haircut and bathed it "I Can't wait until you grow up" said the son to his puppy.

الْقِصَّةُ الْحَادِيَةُ وَالثَّلَاثِينَ

السِّينَمَا

زُرْنَا السِّينَمَا يَوْمَ الْخَمِيسِ الْمَاضِي لِمُشَاهَدَةِ فِيلْمِ الْأَفَنْجَرْزْ الْجَدِيدِ. أَنَا أَحْبَبْتُهُ. كُلُّ مَشْهَدٍ أَبْقَانِي عَلَى أَصَابِعِ قَدَمِي وَمُتَلَهِّفٍ لِمَعْرِفَةِ مَا سَيَحْدُثُ بَعْدَ ذَلِكَ. أَخِي ، عَلَى أَيَّةِ حَالٍ ، لَمْ يَتَمَتَّعْ بِالْفِيلْمِ. نَامَ نِصْفَ سَاعَةٍ فَقَطْ فِي الفِيلْمِ. أَخِي كَانَ يَشْخَرُ بِصَوْتٍ عَالٍ فِي السِّينَمَا الْجَمِيعُ يُمْكِنُ أَنْ يَسْمَعَهُ ، كَانَ يُخَرِّبُ الْفِيلْمَ. أَيْقَظْتُهُ وَهَمَسَتُ "تَوَقَّفَ عَنْ الشَّخِيرِ ، أَنْتَ تَعْطِيلُ الْفِيلْمِ لِلْجَمِيعِ" نَظَرَ حَوْلَهُ وَرَأَى الْعَدِيدَ مِنْ الْوُجُوهِ الْغَاضِبَةِ تُحَدِّقُ فِيهِ. وَقَالَ ، "أَنَا آسِفٌ" ، فِي نَبْرَةٍ مُحْرِجَةٍ.

Story 31

The cinemas

We visited the cinemas last Thursday, to watch the new avenger's movie. I loved it. Each scene kept me on my toes and eager to find out what will happen next. My brother, however, didn't enjoy the movie. He fell asleep only half an hour into the movie. My brother was snoring loudly in the cinema, everybody could hear him, he was ruining the movie. I woke him up and whispered, "stop snoring, you are disrupting the movie for everybody" he looked around him and saw many angry faces staring at him. he said, "I'm sorry", in an embarrassed tone.

الْقِصَّةُ الثَّانِيَةُ وَالثَّلَاثِينَ

الصَّفُّ

وَصَلْتُ إِلَى فَصْلِ الرِّيَاضِيَّاتِ فِي وَقْتٍ مُتَأَخِّرٍ ، كَانَ لَدَيَّ أَسْبَابِي ، وَلَكِنَّ الْمُعَلِّمَ كَانَ بَعِيدًا عَنْ الْإِعْجَابِ. دُونَ أَنْ يَطْلُبَ مِنِّي تَفْسِيرًا ، طَلَبَ مِنِّي أَنْ أَتْرُكَ الْفَصْلَ الدِّرَاسِيَّ لِلْحُضُورِ فِي وَقْتٍ مُتَأَخِّرٍ. هَذَا جَعَلَنِي مُسْتَاءً لِأَنَّنِي جِئْتُ فِي وَقْتٍ مُتَأَخِّرٍ إِلَى الْفَصْلِ بِسَبَبِ بَعْضِ الْأَسْبَابِ الشَّخْصِيَّةِ. اِنْتَظَرْتُ فِي الْمَكْتَبَةِ بِصَبْرٍ لِمُدَّةِ سَاعَةٍ وَاحِدَةٍ ، أَقْرَأُ كِتَابِي الْهَزْلِيَّ ، بَعْدَ انْتِهَاءِ الْفَصْلِ ، ذَهَبْتُ لِلتَّحَدُّثِ مَعَ الْمُعَلِّمِ ، بَعْدَ أَنْ شَرَحْتُ لَهُ لِمَاذَا جِئْتُ فِي وَقْتٍ مُتَأَخِّرٍ جِدًّا ، اِعْتَذَرَ عَلَى الْفَوْرِ وَسَأَلَنِي كَيْفَ يُمْكِنُ أَنْ يَجْعَلَ الْأُمُورَ فِي نِصَابِهَا الصَّحِيحِ. قَبِلْتُ اِعْتِذَارَهُ. بَعْدَ كُلِّ شَيْءٍ ، جَمِيعُنَا نُخْطِئُ، صَحِيحٌ ؟

Story 32

The classroom

I arrived to my maths class late, I had my reasons, but the teacher was far from impressed. Without even asking me for an explanation, he asked me to leave the classroom for coming late. This made me upset because I came late to the classroom because of some personal reasons. I waited in the library patiently for one hour, reading my comic book, after the class finished, I went to speak to the teacher, after I explained to him why I came so late, he immediately apologized and asked me how he could make things right. I accepted his apology. After all, we all make mistakes, right?

الْقِصَّةُ الثَّالِثَةُ وَالثَّلَاثِينَ

طُمُوحَاتٌ

كُلُّنَا لَدَيْنَا طُمُوحَاتُنَا وَرَغَبَاتُنَا فِي الْحَيَاةِ. بَعْضُ النَّاسِ يَعِيشُونَ لِخِدْمَةِ الْآخَرِينَ ، فِي حِينِ أَنَّ النَّاسَ الْآخَرِينَ يُحِبُّونَ الْمُنَافَسَةَ فِي الثَّرْوَةِ ، النَّاسُ الْآخَرِينَ يُحِبُّونَ الْمَزْجَ بَيْنَ الِاثْنَيْنِ. الْحَيَاةُ الْمِثَالِيَّةُ بِالنِّسْبَةِ لِي هِيَ السَّفَرُ إِلَى الْعَالَمِ ، وَالَّذِي لَطَالَمَا أَرَدْتُ الْقِيَامَ بِهِ. وَحَتَّى الْآنَ ، لَمْ أَذْهَبْ إِلَّا إِلَى أَرْبَعَةِ بُلْدَانٍ مُخْتَلِفَةٍ ، هِيَ الدَّانْمَرْكُ وَأَمْرِيكَا وَأَيْرْلَنْدَا وَبَلْجِيكَا. أُرِيدُ السَّفَرَ إِلَى جَنُوبِ شَرْقِ آسْيَا ، بُلْدَانٌ مِثْلَ إِنْدُونِيسْيَا وَمَالِيزْيَا وَسَنْغَافُورَةْ وَتَايْلَنْدَ. أُحِبُّ الْمَشَاهِدَ الْجَمِيلَةَ فِي هَذِهِ الْبُلْدَانِ ، الشَّوَاطِئُ الشَّلَالَاتُ النَّاسُ الرَّقِيقَةِ وَالْمُبْتَهِجَةِ. رُبَّمَا أُرِيدُ أَنْ أُقِيمَ فِي أَحَدِ هَذِهِ ، الْبُلْدَانِ فِي الْمُسْتَقْبَلِ ، إِنْ شَاءَ اللهُ

Story 33

Ambitions

We all have our ambitions and desires in life. Some people live to serve others, while other people like to compete in wealth, other people like to mix both. An ideal life for me would be to travel the world, which I have always wanted to do. So far, I have only been to four different countries, Denmark, America, Ireland and Belgium. I want to travel to southeast Asia, countries like Indonesia, Malaysia, Singapore and Thailand. I love the beautiful sights in these countries, the beaches, the waterfalls, the kind and cheerful people. Perhaps I would want to reside in one of these countries in the future, God willing.

الْقِصَّةُ الرَّابِعَةُ وَالثَّلَاثِينَ

أَرَقٌ

أَتَغَيّبُ عَنِ اللَّيَالِي عِنْدَمَا كُنْتُ أَحْصُلُ عَلَى ثَمَانِ سَاعَاتِ نَوْمٍ ، حَيْثُ جَسَدِي كَانَ يَسْتَيْقِظُ مُنْعِشَ ، مُرْتَاحٌ وَمُسْتَعِدٌّ لِبَدْءِ الْيَوْمِ. مُنْذُ أَنْ أَصْبَحْتُ أَرِقًا ، حَيَاتِي إِنْقَلَبَتْ رَأْساً عَلَى عَقِبٍ. أَنَا مُتْعِبٌ جِدًّا طَوَالَ النَّهَارِ ، النَّوْمُ قَلِيلٌ خِلَالَ اللَّيْلِ ، أَفْتَقِرُ إِلَى الدَّافِعِ أَوْ الرَّغْبَةِ فِي الْقِيَامِ بِأَيِّ شَيْءٍ ، وَالشُّعُورُ بِالسُّوءِ تُجَاهَ نَفْسِي. أَتَسَاءَلُ مَا سَبَبُ هَذِهِ الْفَوْضَى. هُوَ مَا كَانَ يَكُونُ مِثْلَ هَذَا. لَقَدْ جَرَّبْتُ كُلَّ شَيْءٍ ، مِنْ الْحُبُوبِ الْمُنَوِّمَةِ إِلَى الْعِلَاجَاتِ الطَّبِيعِيَّةِ وَجَمِيعِ أَشْيَاءِ نَظَافَةِ النَّوْمِ نَسْمَعُ عَنْهَا. بِالْأَمْسِ ، أُوْصِيْتُ بِطَبِيبٍ رَفِيعِ الْجَوْدَةِ. أَتَمَنَّى بِأَنَّهُ يُمْكِنُ أَنْ يُسَاعِدَنِي.

Story 34

My insomnia

I miss the nights when I used to get eight hours of sleep, where my body would wake up refreshed, relaxed and ready to start the day. Ever since I have become an insomniac, my life has turned upside down. I'm very tired throughout the day, sleep little during the night, lack motivation or desire to do anything, and feel bad about myself. I wonder what caused this mess. It never used to be like this. I've tried everything, from sleeping pills to natural remedies and all of the sleep hygiene stuff we hear about. Yesterday, I was recommended a top-quality doctor. I hope he can help me out.

الْقِصَّةُ الْخَامِسَةُ وَالثَّلَاثِينَ

حُلْمُ أَحْمَدَ

بَدَأَ أَحْمَدُ شَرِكَتَهُ عَلَى الْإِنْتَرْنِتْ الْعَامَ الْمَاضِيَ. الْيَوْمَ هُوَ أَخِيرًا يَحْصُلُ عَلَى تَرْكِ عَمَلِهِ. كَانَ سَعِيدًا جِدًّا كَمَا كَانَ يَعْمَلُ بِجِدٍّ عَلَى ذَلِكَ. يَبِيعُ أَحْمَدُ مَجْمُوعَةً مِنْ الْمُنْتَجَاتِ الرَّقْمِيَّةِ مِنْ كُتُبٍ، وَدَوْرَاتٍ وَ الْكُتُبِ الصَّوْتِيَّةِ إِلَى مُنْتَجَاتٍ مَادِّيَّةٍ مِنْ مَلَابِسٍ وَمُلْحَقَاتٍ وَأَجْهِزَةٍ كَهْرَبَائِيَّةٍ. وَيُخَطِّطُ أَحْمَدُ لِتَوْسِيعِ عَلَامَتِهِ التِّجَارِيَّةِ ؛ يُرِيدُ أَنْ يَأْخُذَ أَعْمَالَهُ إِلَى الْحُدُودِ الدَّوْلِيَّةِ. وَيَعْتَزِمَ الدُّخُولَ إِلَى الْمَنْطِقَةِ الْآسْيَوِيَّةِ وَالْأَفْرِيقِيَّةِ. وَهُوَ يُخَطِّطُ لِتَغْيِيرِ حَيَاةِ النَّاسِ ، وَتَزْوِيدِهِمْ بِالْقِيمَةِ وَ لِإِيجَادِ فُرَصِ عَمَلٍ لِأَقَلِّ النَّاسِ حَظًّا.

Story 35

Ahmed's dream

Ahmed started his online business last year. Today he finally gets to quit his job. He was so happy as he worked so hard on it. All the hard work paid off. Ahmed sells a range of products, from digital products such as books, courses and audiobooks, to physical products such as clothes, accessories and electrical appliances. Ahmed plans to expand his brand; he wants to take his business into international boundaries. He intends to step into the Asian and African region. He plans to change people's lives, provide them with value and create jobs for the less fortunate.

الْقِصَّةُ السَّادِسَةُ وَالثَّلَاثِينَ

إِعَادَةُ اتِّحَادِ الْأُسْرَةِ

لَقَدْ مَرَّتْ ثَلَاثُ سَنَوَاتٍ مُنْذُ آخِرِ مَرَّةٍ رَأَى فِيهَا مَارْكُوسْ عَائِلَتَهُ. غَادَرَ الْمَمْلَكَةَ الْمُتَّحِدَةَ لِلْعَمَلِ فِي الْخَارِجِ فِي الْإِمَارَاتِ الْعَرَبِيَّةِ الْمُتَّحِدَةِ. فِي نِهَايَةِ هَذَا الْأُسْبُوعِ ، كَانَ يَنْوِي الْعَوْدَةَ إِلَى الْمَمْلَكَةِ الْمُتَّحِدَةِ لِلَمِّ شَمْلٍ مَعَ عَائِلَتِهِ. بِمَا أَنَّهُ لَمْ يَزُرْهُمْ لِأَكْثَرِ مِنْ ثَلَاثِ سَنَوَاتٍ ، لَدَيْهِ الْكَثِيرُ مِنْ التَّسَوُّقِ لِلْقِيَامِ بِهِ. يَحْتَاجُ لِشِرَاءِ الْهَدَايَا لِعَائِلَتِهِ وَأَصْدِقَائِهِ. يَحْتَاجُ أَيْضًا إِلَى فَرْزِ تَرْتِيبَاتِ جُلُوسِهِ عَلَى مَتْنِ الطَّائِرَةِ. مَارْكُوسْ يُفَضِّلُ مَقَاعِدَ النَّافِذَةِ. يُحِبُّ أَنْ يَنْظُرَ إِلَى الْغُيُومِ وَالسَّمَاءِ. إِنَّهُمْ يَبْهَرُوْنَهُ. مِنَ الْمُتَوَقَّعِ أَنْ يَهْبِطَ مَارْكُوسْ فِي الْمَمْلَكَةِ الْمُتَّحِدَةِ فِي الصَّبَاحِ. ثُمَّ يُخَطِّطُ لِأَخْذِ سَيَّارَةِ أُجْرَةٍ لِلْمَنْزِلِ وَمُفَاجَأَةِ عَائِلَتِهِ.

Story 36

The family re-union

It had been three years since Marcus last saw his family. He left the UK to work abroad in the United Arab Emirates. This weekend, he intends to travel back to the UK to reunite with his family. Since he hasn't visited them for over three years, he has a lot of shopping to do. He needs to buy gifts for his family and friends. He also needs to sort out his seating arrangements on the plane. Marcus prefers the window seats. He likes to look at the clouds and skies. They fascinate him. Marcus is projected to land in the UK in the morning. He then plans to take a taxi home and surprise his family.

الْقِصَّةُ السَّابِعَةُ وَالثَّلَاثِين

الْفَتَى الْيَتِيمُ

أَتَذَكَّرُ عِنْدَمَا أَيْتَمْنَا أَنَا وَزَوْجَتِي صَّبِيٌّ صَغِيرٌ قَبْلَ عَشْرِ سَنَوَاتٍ تَقْرِيبًا. مُنْذُ ذَلِكَ الْحِينِ ، كَانَ يَعِيشُ مَعَنَا فِي وِئَامٍ. عَلَى الرَّغْمِ مِنْ أَنَّهُ لَيْسَ اِبْنَنَا الْبَيُولُوجِيّ ، نُعَامِلُهُ كَمَا هُوَ. لَطَالَمَا أَرَدْنَا أَطْفَالَ كَزَوْجَيْنِ. لِسُوءِ الْحَظِّ نَحْنُ لَمْ نَكُنْ مُبَارَكِيْنَ بِأَيّ مِنّا ، وَلَكِنَّ هَذَا لَمْ يَمْنَعْنَا مِنْ تَيْتِيمِ طِفْلٍ صَغِيرٍ. غَدًا الذِّكْرَى السَّنَوِيَّةَ الْعَشْرَ لِطِفْلِنَا الْيَتِيمِ. لَقَدْ كَبُرَ الْآنَ، يَتَحَدَّثُ بِطَلَاقَةٍ .يَذْهَبُ إِلَى الْمَدْرَسَةِ ، وَهُوَ طِفْلٌ ذَكِيٌّ. هُوَ حَقًّاً وَاحِدٌ مِنّا

Story 37

The orphaned boy

I remember when me and my wife orphaned a young boy nearly ten years ago. Since then, he has been living with us in harmony. Even though he is not our biological son, we treat him like he is. We always wanted children as a couple. Unfortunately, we weren't blessed with any of our own, but that didn't stop us from orphaning a young child. Tomorrow is our ten-year anniversary with our orphaned child. He is so grown up now, he speaks fluently, goes to school, and is a clever child. He is truly one of our own.

الْقِصَّةُ الثَّامِنَةُ وَالثَّلَاثِين

نَدْبَتِي

يَسْأَلُنِي النَّاسُ دَائِمًا عَنْ النَّدْبَةِ عَلَى ذِرَاعِي. عَلَى أَيَّةِ حَالٍ ، أَنَا لَا أُحِبُّ الْكَلَامَ عَنْهَا. بِالنِّسْبَةِ لِلْعَدِيدِ مِنْ النَّاسِ ، النُّدُوبُ يُمْكِنُ أَنْ تُشْبِهَ عِدَّةَ أَشْيَاءَ ، وَلَكِنَّ نُدُوبِي تُشْبِهُ الِاكْتِئَابَ الْخَوْفَ وَالْقَلَقَ. لَنْ أَنْسَى أَبَداً لَيْلَةَ الْحَادِثِ ، حَيْثُ كُنْتُ النَّاجِيَ الْوَحِيدَ فِي حَادِثِ سَيَّارَةٍ ، لَيْلَةَ وَفَاةِ أَصْدِقَائِي الثَّلَاثَةِ الْمَحْبُوبِينَ لِلْأَسَفِ. أَنَا لَنْ أَفْهَمَهُ. لِمَاذَا عَلَى النَّاسِ الْقِيَادَةُ بِتَهَوُّرٍ ؟ لِمَاذَا لَا يُمْكِنُنَا أَنْ نَكُونَ أَكْثَرَ وَعْيًا مِنْ النَّاسِ الْآخَرِينَ مِنْ حَوْلِنَا ؟ لِمَاذَا كَانَ عَلَيْهِ أَنْ يَنْتَهِيَ بِهَذِهِ الطَّرِيقَةِ ؟ مَا زِلْتُ أَجِدُ نَفْسِي الذَّهَابَ لِجَلَسَاتِ الْعِلَاجِ مِنْ وَقْتٍ لِآخَرَ كُلَّمَا أَشْعُرُ بِالْحُزْنِ وَ ذِكْرَيَاتِ حَوْلَ تِلْكَ اللَّيْلَةِ. هَذِهِ الْمَشَاعِرُ سَتَبْقَى لِبَقِيَّةِ حَيَاتِي.

Story 38

My scar

People always ask me about the scar on my arm. However, I don't like to speak about it. For many people, scars can resemble several things, but my scars resemble depression, fear, and anxiety. I will never forget the night of the accident, where I was the only survivor in a car crash, the night my three beloved friends sadly passed away. I will never understand it. Why do people have to drive so recklessly? Why can't we be more mindful of other people around us? Why did it have to end this way? I still find myself going to therapy sessions from time to time whenever I feel sad and have flashbacks about that night. These feelings will undoubtedly remain for the rest of my life.

الْقِصَّةُ التَّاسِعَةُ وَالثَّلَاثِينَ

الرَّجُلُ الْبَرِيءُ

لَقَدْ مَرَّ عَامَانِ مُنْذُ أَنْ دَخَلَ جُونُ السِّجْنَ بِطَرِيقِ الْخَطَأِ بِسَبَبِ جَرِيمَةٍ لَمْ يَرْتَكِبْهَا قَطُّ. كَيْفَ الشُّرْطَةَ تَحْصُلُ عَلَيْهِ خَاطِئٌ جِدًّاً ؟ أَلَمْ تَنْظُرْ الْمَحْكَمَةُ إِلَى الْأَدِلَّةِ ؟ مُنْذُ الْحُكْمِ عَلَى جُونْ ، كَانَتْ عَائِلَةُ جُونْ تَحْتَ قَدْرٍ كَبِيرٍ مِنْ الْإِجْهَادِ ، وَأُمُّ جُونْ وَوَالِدُهُ كَانَ لَدَيْهِم عِدَّةُ لَيَالِيَ مُؤَرِّقَةٍ وَخَسِرَ إِخْوَتُهُ شَقِيقَهُمْ الْأَكْبَرَ. فَتَحَتْ الْعَائِلَةُ نِدَاءً لِابْنِهِمْ. إِنّ النِّدَاءَ أَنْ يَهْبِطَ عُطْلَةَ نِهَايَةِ الْأُسْبُوعِ هَذِهِ. وَالِدَةُ جُونْ كَانَتْ تُعِدُّ كُلَّ الْأَدِلَّةِ خِلَالَ الشَّهْرَيْنِ الْمَاضِيَيْنِ ، وَهِيَ مُصَمِّمَةٌ عَلَى الْفَوْزِ بِالْقَضِيَّةِ. إِنَّهَا تَفْتَقِدُ اِبْنَهَا.

Story 39

The innocent man

It has been two years since John was wrongfully admitted into prison for a crime he never committed. How could the police get it so wrong? did the court not look at the evidence? Since John has been sentenced, John's family has been under a great deal of stress, John's mother and father have had multiple sleepless nights, and his brothers have lost their elder brother. The family opened up an appeal for their son. The appeal is to go down this weekend. John's mother has been preparing all of the pieces of evidence for the last two months, and she's determined to win the case. She misses her son.

الْقِصَّةُ الْأَرْبَعِينَ

بِرِيطَانْيَا لَدَيْهَا الْمَوْهِبَةُ

كَانَتْ مُغَنِّيَةٌ شَابَّةٌ مِنْ وَاتْفُورْدْ سَعِيدَةً عِنْدَمَا حَصَلَتْ عَلَى فُرْصَةِ الْمُشَارَكَةِ فِي بِرِيطَانْيَا لَدَيْهَا مَوْهِبَةٌ. كَانَتْ تُعْتَبَرُ مَوْهُوبَةً لِلْغَايَةِ مِنْ قِبَلِ مُجْتَمَعِهَا الْمَحَلِّيِّ ، وَكَانَتْ تَنْتَظِرُ فُرْصَةً كَهَذِهِ لِفَتْرَةٍ طَوِيلَةٍ. شَعَرَتْ بِمَسْؤُولِيَّةٍ كَبِيرَةٍ عَلَى عَاتِقِهَا لِسَدَادِ الْإِيمَانِ الَّذِي وَضَعَهُ الْمُجْتَمَعُ فِيهَا. وَمَعَ ذَلِكَ ، فَإِنَّ فُرَصَهَا دُمِّرَتْ عِنْدَمَا تَعَطَّلَتْ سَيَّارَتُهَا فِي الطَّرِيقِ إِلَى الْمُنَافَسَةِ. عَلَى الرَّغْمِ مِنْ كُلِّ مَا حَدَثَ ، إِنَّهَا لَا تَزَالُ قَادِرَةً عَلَى الْفَوْزِ فِي الْمُنَافَسَةِ بِأَكْمَلِهَا. ذَهَبَتْ فِي وَقْتٍ لَاحِقٍ لِتُصْبِحَ مُغَنِّيَةً عَالَمِيَّةً!

Story 40

Britain's got talent

A young singer from Watford was delighted when she got the chance to participate in Britain's got talent. She was regarded as highly talented by her local community, and she'd been waiting for an opportunity like this for a long time. She felt a huge responsibility on her shoulders to repay the faith that the community put in her. However, her chances became destroyed when her car broke down on the way to the competition. Despite everything that had happened, she still managed to win the whole competition. She later went on to become a global singer!

الْقِصَّةُ الْحَادِيَةُ وَالْأَرْبَعِينَ

الرَّجُلُ الْجَشَعُ

كَانَ هُنَاكَ رَجُلٌ جَشِعٌ يُسَمَّى فِيكْتُورْ ، كَانَ يَعِيشُ فِي بَلْدَةٍ صَغِيرَةٍ فِي جَنُوبِ الْبِلَادِ. كَانَ رَجُلٌ غَنِيٌّ ، يَمْتَلِكُ الْكَثِيرَ مِنْ الذَّهَبِ وَالْمُجَوْهَرَاتِ. ذَاتَ يَوْمٍ عَثَرَ عَلَى سَيِّدَةٍ. كَانَتْ عَالِقَةً فِي شَجَرَةٍ وَلَمْ تَسْتَطِعْ الْخُرُوجَ. الرَّجُلُ الْجَشِعَ سَاعَدَهَا ، لَكِنَّهُ طَلَبَ خِدْمَةً بِالْمُقَابِلِ. كَانَتْ السَّيِّدَةُ فَقِيرَةً لِلْغَايَةِ وَلَمْ يَكُنْ لَدَيْهَا شَيْءٌ تُعْطِيهِ لِلرَّجُلِ الْجَشَعَ. أَخَذَ آخِرَ كَمِّيَّةٍ مِنْ الْمَالِ الَذِي كَانَ بِحَوْزَتِهَا. هَذَا تَرَكَهَا مَكْسُورَةَ الْقَلْبِ

Story 41

The Greedy man

There was a greedy man named Victor, who was living in a small town in the south of the country. He was a rich man. He possessed many gold and jewellery. One day he stumbled across a lady. She was stuck in a tree and couldn't come out. The greedy man helped her out, but he asked for a favor in return. The lady was very poor and had nothing to give to the greedy man. In the end, he took the last bit of money that she had. This left her heartbroken.

الْقِصَّةُ الثَّانِيَةُ وَالْأَرْبَعِينَ

النَّمْلَةُ

.فِي يَوْمِ صَيْفٍ حَارٍّ ، كَانَتْ النَّمْلَةُ تَتَجَوَّلُ بِلَا كَلَلٍ بَحْثًا عَنْ بَعْضِ الْمَاءِ .النَّمْلَةُ كَانَتْ تَتَقَطَّرُ فِي الْعَرَقِ. فَجْأَةً ، بَعْدَ أَنْ كَانَتْ تَتَجَوَّلُ لِعِدَّةِ سَاعَاتٍ ، أَتَتْ النَّمْلَةُ عَبْرَ نَهْرٍ كَبِيرٍ. أَضَاءَتْ عُيُونُ النَّمْلَةِ فَجْأَةً. النَّمْلَةُ كَانَتْ مَسْرُورَةً لِرُؤْيَتِهَا. صَعِدَتْ النَّمْلَةُ نَحْوَ النَّهْرِ بِمُسَاعَدَةِ صَخْرَةٍ صَغِيرَةٍ لِسُوءِ الْحَظِّ ، اِنْزَلَقَتْ النَّمْلَةُ وَسَقَطَتْ بِقُوَّةٍ فِي النَّهْرِ. بَيْنَمَا هَذَا كَانَ يَحْدُثُ كَانَ هُنَاكَ حَمَامَةٌ قَرِيبَةٌ الَّتِي كَانَتْ تُرَاقِبُ الْوَضْعَ. عِنْدَمَا أَدْرَكَتْ الْحَمَامَةُ أَنَّ النَّمْلَةَ قَدْ غَرِقَتْ ، سَاعَدَتْ عَلَى الْفَوْرِ النَّمْلَةِ. "لَقَدْ أَنْقَذْتِ .حَيَاتِي" قَالَتْ النَّمْلَةُ

Story 42

The ant

On a hot summer's day, an ant was walking around tirelessly in search of some water. The ant was dripping in sweat. Suddenly, after it was walking around for multiple hours, the ant came across a large river. The ants' eyes suddenly lit up. The ant was delighted to see it. The ant climbed up towards the river with the help of a small rock. Unfortunately, the ant slipped and fell vigorously into the river. Whilst this was happening, there was a dove nearby who was observing the situation. When the dove realized that the ant had sunk, she immediately helped the ant. "Thank you. You saved my life," said the ant.

الْقِصَّةُ الثَّالِثَةُ وَالْأَرْبَعِينَ

الدُّبْ

كَانَتْ لَيْلَةً هَادِئَةً مُظْلِمَةً عِنْدَمَا كَانَتْ جُولِي وَأَنْثَا يَسِيرَانِ عَلَى طُولِ غَابَةٍ خَطِرَةٍ. قَالَتْ جُولِي "رُبَّمَا لَمْ يَكُنْ عَلَيْنَا أَخْذُ هَذَا الطَّرِيقِ لِلْمَنْزِلِ!" بِلَهْجَةٍ مُخِيفَةٍ وَقَلِقَةٍ. أَجَابَتْ أَنْثَا:" لَقَدْ فَاتَ الْأَوَانُ الْآنَ ، لَا يُمْكِنُنَا الْعَوْدَةُ مَرَّةً أُخْرَى". فَجْأَةً ، كَمَا كَانَتَا تُطَارِدَانِ الْغَابَةَ ، رَأَتَا دُبًّا. أَصْبَحَتْ الْفَتَاتَانِ خَائِفَتَانِ جِدًّاً ، لِذَا رَكَضَتَا نَحْوَ أَقْرَبِ شَجَرَةٍ قَرِيبَةٍ. جُولِيَا تَمَكَّنَتْ مِنْ تَسَلُّقِ الشَّجَرَةِ ، بَيْنَمَا أَنَّثَا لَمْ تَعْرِفْ كَيْفَ تَتَسَلَّقُ الشَّجَرَةَ. الْوَقْتُ كَانَ يَمْضِي ، وَبَدَأَتْ بِالذُّعْرِ. قَرَّرَتْ أَنْ تَسْتَلْقِيَ عَلَى الْأَرْضِ ، تَتَظَاهَرُ بِأَنَّهَا مَيِّتَةً. الدُّبُ اِقْتَرَبَ مِنْ أُنْثَا. ظَنَّ الدُّبُ أَنَّهَا مَيِّتَةً ، لِذَا لَمْ يُسَبِّبْ لَهَا أَيَّ أَذَى عَلَى الْإِطْلَاق

Story 43

The Bear

It was a dark, quiet night when Julie and Antha were walking along a dangerous forest. "We probably shouldn't have taken this route home!" said Julie, in a scary and anxious tone. Antha replied, "it's too late now, we can't head back any more". suddenly, as they were striding along the jungle, they saw a bear. The two girls became very scared, so they ran towards the closest tree nearby. Julia managed to climb the tree, while Antha didn't know how to climb the tree. Time was ticking, and she started to panic. She decided to lay on the ground, pretending to be dead. The bear approached Antha. The bear thought she was dead, so he caused her no harm at all.

الْقِصَّةُ الرَّابِعَةُ وَالْأَرْبَعِينَ

الْأَسَدُ الْجَائِعُ

لَقَدْ كَانَ يَوْماً سَاخِناً فِي الْأَرْضِ الْعُشْبِيَّةِ عِنْدَمَا بَدَأَ بَطْنُ الْأَسَدِ بِالتَّدَحْرُجِ. وَبَدَأَ عَلَى الْفَوْرِ فِي الْبَحْثِ عَنْ الطَّعَامِ فِي مَكَانٍ قَرِيبٍ. بَعْدَ ، فَتْرَةٍ قَلِيلَةٍ ، وَجَدَ أَرْنَبٌ صَغِيرٌ كَانَ يَتَجَوَّلُ مِنْ تِلْقَاءِ نَفْسِهِ. عَلَى أَيَّةِ حَالٍ قَرَّرَ أَنْ لَا يَأْكُلَ الْأَرْنَبَ. وَقَالَ الْأَسَدُ "لَا يُمْكِنُ لِأَرْنَبٍ صَغِيرٍ أَنْ يُرْضِيَ جُوعِي" ، ثُمَّ وَاصَلَ بَحْثَهُ. ثُمَّ صَادَفَ الْغَزْلَانَ "هَذَا أَشْبَهُ بِذَلِكَ" ، وَقَالَ الْأَسَدُ بِلَهْجَةٍ مُتَحَمِّسَةٍ. لَقَدْ قَامَ الْأَسَدُ بِمُطَارَدَةِ الْأَيْلِ بِعُدْوَانِيَّةٍ ؛ وَمَعَ ذَلِكَ سُرْعَانَ مَا أَدْرَكَ الْأَسَدُ أَنَّهُ لَنْ يُوَاكِبَ الْغَزَالَ بِسَبَبِ كَمْ كَانَ جَائِعًا ، وَالْحَرَارَةُ. هَذَا تَرَكَ الْأَسَدُ فِي مِزَاجٍ حَزِينٍ. بَقِيَ جَائِعاً لِبَقِيَّةِ ذَلِكَ الْيَوْمِ.

Story 44

The hungry lion

It was a hot day in the Greenland when the lion's belly began rumbling. He immediately began hunting for food nearby. After a little while, he found a small hare that was roaming around on its own. However, he decided not to eat the hare. The lion said, "a small hare cannot satisfy my hunger," and then he continued his search. He then came across a deer "this is more like it!" said the lion in an enthusiastic tone. The lion aggressively chased the deer; however, the lion quickly realized that he wouldn't keep up with the deer because of how hungry he was and the heat. This left the lion in a sad mood. He stayed hungry for the remainder of that day.

الْقِصَّةُ الْخَامِسَةُ وَالْأَرْبَعِينَ

حَفْلُ زِفَافِ أَخِي

غَدًا هُوَ زِفَافُ أَخِي. عَائِلَتُنَا سَعِيدَةٌ جِدًّاً لِأَجْلِهِ. لَقَدْ كَانَ يَبْحَثُ عَنْ زَوْجَةٍ لِفَتْرَةٍ طَوِيلَةٍ. الِانْتِظَارُ كَانَ يَسْتَحِقُّ ذَلِكَ. خَطِيبَتُهُ جَمِيلَةٌ. لَدَيْهَا شَعْرٌ مُجْعِدٌ طَوِيلٌ ، عُيُونٌ زَرْقَاءُ ، وَابْتِسَامَةٌ رَائِعَةٌ. كَانَ هُنَاكَ مُشْكِلَةٌ وَاحِدَةٌ ، لَمْ يَكُنْ لَدَيَّ فُسْتَانٌ لِلزِّفَافِ .كَيْفَ يُمْكِنُنِي تَرْكُهُ فِي هَذَا الْوَقْتِ الْمُتَأَخِّرِ ؟ أَنَا مُصَمِّمَةٌ عَلَى إِيجَادِ فُسْتَانٍ فِي الْوَقْتِ الْمُنَاسِبِ لِزِفَافِ إِخْوَتِي. لَا يُمْكِنُنِي أَنْ أَكُونَ الْوَحِيدَ بِدُونِ فُسْتَانٍ. ذَلِكَ سَيَكُونُ إِحْرَاجاً إِلَى أَخِّي وَعَائِلَتِي. فِي وَقْتٍ لَاحِقٍ مِنْ الْيَوْمِ ، أَنَا سَأَذْهَبُ لِزِيَارَةِ صَالُونِ الزِّفَافِ الْمَحَلِّيِّ. آمُلُ أَنْ أَجِدَ فُسْتَانً فِي الْوَقْتِ الْمُنَاسِبِ لِزِفَافِ إِخْوَتِي

Story 45

My brother's wedding

Tomorrow is my brother's wedding. Our family is so happy for him. He has been searching for a wife for a long time. The wait was worth it, though. His fiancée is beautiful. She has long curly hair, blue eyes, and a gorgeous smile. There was one problem, though. I didn't have a dress for the wedding, how could I possibly leave it this late? I am determined to find a dress in time for my brothers' wedding. I can't be the only one without a dress. That would be an embarrassment to my brother and my family. Later on in the day, I'm going to visit a local bridal salon. I hope to find a dress in time for my brothers' wedding.

الْقِصَّةُ السَّادِسَةُ وَالْأَرْبَعِينَ

الْإِجْهَاضُ

صَدِيقَتِي الْمُقَرَّبَةُ ، إِيلَا ، فَقَدَتْ طِفْلاً حَدِيثاً بِسَبَبِ الْإِجْهَاضِ. الْأَسَابِيعَ الْقَلِيلَةَ الْمَاضِيَةَ كَانَتْ قَاسِيَةً عَلَيْهَا وَعَلَى الْعَائِلَةِ. لَقَدْ أَثَّرتْ عَلَيَّ أَيْضاً. أَنَا لَا أَتَمَنَّى أَلَمَ الْإِجْهَاضِ لِأَيِّ شَخْصٍ. مُؤَخَّراً ، الْحَيَاةُ الزَّوْجِيَّةُ لِصَدِيقَتِي تَغَيَّرَتْ. زَوْجُ صَدِيقَتِي، الَّذِي كَانَ عَادَةً أَكْثَرَ كَلَامًا مِنْ الِاثْنَيْنِ ، كَانَ يَقْضِي الْكَثِيرَ مِنْ الْوَقْتِ لِوَحْدِهِ ، يَحْزَنُ عَلَى مَوْتِ حَيَاةِ بِنْتِهِ. مِنْ نَاحِيَةٍ أُخْرَى أَخَذَتْ إِيلَا بِضْعَةَ أَشْهُرٍ مِنْ الْعَمَلِ. لَيْسَ هُنَاكَ يَوْمٌ يَمُرُّ حَيْثُ لَا تُفَكِّرُ فِي اِبْنَتِهَا الصَّغِيرَةِ. إِيلَا تَأْمُلُ أَنْ تَلْتَقِيَ يَوْماً مَا بِابْنَتِهَا الصَّغِيرَةِ الْجَمِيلَةِ. رُبَّمَا فِي الْجَنَّةِ

Story 46

The miscarriage

My best friend, Ella, has recently lost a newborn child by miscarriage. The last few weeks have been very tough on her and the family. It has also affected me, though. I don't wish the pain of a miscarriage to anybody. Recently, my friends' marriage life has changed. My friends' husband, who was usually the more talkative one out of the two, has been spending a lot of time on his own, grieving for the death of his daughters' life. On the other hand, Ella has taken a few months off work. There isn't a day that goes by where she doesn't think about her little daughter. Ella hopes to one day meet her beautiful little daughter, in heaven perhaps.

الْقِصَّةُ السَّابِعَةُ وَالْأَرْبَعِينَ

بَطَلَنَا

آدَمُ هُوَ بَطَلٌ فِي نَظَرِي ، أَنْهَى مُؤَخَّرًا بَرْنَامِجَهُ الْجَامِعِيَّ ، وَكَانَ مِنْ الْمُتَوَقَّعِ أَنْ يَذْهَبَ إِلَى وَاحِدَةٍ مِنْ أَفْضَلِ الْجَامِعَاتِ فِي الْبِلَادِ حَتَّى تَمَّ الْهُجُومُ عَلَى مَسْقَطِ رَأْسِهِ الْمَعْزُولِ مِنْ الْعَدَمِ. آدَمُ قَرَّرَ حِمَايَةَ مَدِينَتِهِ وَعَائِلَتِهِ. لَقَدْ ضَحَّى بِدِرَاسَاتِهِ. آدَمُ قَرَّرَ الْإِنْضِمَامَ لِلْجَيْشِ. كَانَ مَذْعُوراً لِأَنَّهُ لَمْ يَكُنْ لَدَيْهِ أَيِّ تَجْرِبَةٍ سَابِقَةٍ. وَمَعَ ذَلِكَ ، هَذَا لَمْ يُوقِفْ آدَمُ. أَصْبَحَ عُضْوًا قِيَمًا فِي الْفَرِيقِ مِنْ الْجَيْشِ ، مُسَاعَدَتَهُمْ مَعَ اسْتِرَاتِيجِيَّتِهِمْ ، كُلُّ ذَلِكَ بِفَضْلِ رُؤْيَتِهِ الْعِلْمِيَّةِ. قَدَّرَتْ الْبَلْدَةُ مَا فَعَلَهُ آدَمُ وَبَقِيَّةُ الْجَيْشِ لَهُمْ. قَامُوا بِتَرْتِيبِ حَفْلَةٍ كَبِيرَةٍ لَهُمْ بَعْدَ اِنْتِهَاءِ الْحَرْبِ.

Story 47

Our Hero

Adam is a hero in my sight, he recently finished his college program, and he was projected to go to one of the best universities in the country until his isolated hometown was attacked out of nowhere. Adam Decided to protect his town and his family. He sacrificed his studies. Adam decided to join the army. He was terrified as he didn't have any prior experience. However, that didn't stop Adam. He became a valuable team member of the army, helping them with their strategy, all thanks to his scientific insight. The town really appreciated what Adam and the rest of the army had done for them. They arranged a large party for them after the war was finished.

الْقِصَّةُ الثَّامِنَةُ وَالْأَرْبَعِينَ

عَمَلِيَّةُ الْإِخْتِطَافِ

اِبْنُ رَئِيسِ الْوُزَرَاءُ اخْتُطِفَ بَعْدَ ظُهْرِ الْيَوْمِ. وَصَلَتْ الْأَخْبَارُ إِلَى الْجُمْهُورِ فِي غُضُونِ دَقَائِقَ مِنْ الْأَحْدَاثِ الَّتِي تَكْتَشِفُ. وَكَانَ طَاقَمُ الْكَامِيرَا وَمَنَافِذُ الْأَخْبَارِ يُحِيطُ بِمَقَرِّ إِقَامَةِ رَئِيسِ الْوُزَرَاءِ. الْبَلَدُ كُلُّهُ كَانَ فِي حَالَةِ صَدْمَةٍ. مَنْ يُمْكِنُهُ أَنْ يَخْتَطِفَ اِبْنُ رَئِيسِ الْوُزَرَاءِ ؟ الْحُكُومَةُ وَضَعَتْ كُلَّ شَيْءٍ عَلَى وَقْفَةٍ. كَانَتْ الشُّرْطَةُ تَبْحَثُ عَنْ الْفَتَى الْمِسْكِينِ فِي كُلِّ أَنْحَاءِ الْبِلَادِ .لِمُدَّةِ خَمْسِ سَاعَاتٍ الْآنَ ؛ غَيْرَ أَنَّهُ لَمْ يَتِمَّ الْعُثُورُ عَلَى أَيِّ شَيْءٍ حَتَّى الْآنَ رَئِيسُ الْوُزَرَاءِ بَدَأَ يَفْقِدُ الْأَمَلَ. بَيْنَمَا كَانَ يُلْقِي خِطَابَهُ الْعَامَّ ، لَمْ يَسْتَطِعْ أَنْ يَتَرَاجَعَ عَنْ الدُّمُوعِ ، بَيْنَمَا يَقُولُ، أَرْجُوكَ أَعِدَّ إِبْنِي! أَرْجُوكَ أَعِدَّ إِبْنِي

Story 48

The kidnapping

The prime ministers' son was kidnapped this afternoon. The news reached the public within minutes of the events unfolding. The camera crew and news outlets were surrounding the residence of the prime minister. The whole country was in a state of shock. Who could have possibly kidnapped the prime ministers' son? The government put everything on pause. The police have been searching for the poor boy all over the country for five hours now; however, nothing has been found yet. The prime minister is starting to lose hope. Whilst he was delivering his public speech, he couldn't hold back on the tears, whilst saying, "please bring my son back! please bring my son back!"

الْقِصَّةُ التَّاسِعَةُ وَالْأَرْبَعِينَ

عَدَاوَةُ الْمَدْرَسَةِ الثَّانَوِيَّةِ

كَانَ دِيكْلَانْ وَبِنْ أَفْضَلَ الْأَصْدِقَاءِ فِي الْمَدْرَسَةِ الثَّانَوِيَّةِ. فَعَلُوا كُلَّ شَيْءٍ مَعًا ، ذَهَبَا لِتَنَاوُلِ الطَّعَامِ مَعًا ، أَخَذَا دُرُوسَهُمَا مَعًا ، وَحَتَّى أَخَذَا نَفْسَ الطَّرِيقِ المَنْزِلِ مَعًا. فَجْأَةً، تَوَقَّفَا عَنْ الْكَلَامِ بَعْدَ أَنْ كَانَ بَيْنَهُمَا نِزَاعٌ. لَمْ يَتَحَدَّثَا مَعَ بَعْضِهِمَا الْبَعْضَ لِأَكْثَرَ مِنْ عَامَيْنِ. بِالْأَمْسِ ، جَاءَ عَبْرَ بَعْضِهِمَا الْبَعْضُ عَلَى نَفْسِ الرِّحْلَةِ الدَّوْلِيَّةِ. كَانَ مِنْ الْمُحْرِجِ لِكِلَيْهِمَا. لَمْ يَقُولَا كَلِمَةً لِبَعْضِهِمَا الْبَعْضِ لِعِدَّةِ سَاعَاتٍ حَتَّى اِقْتَرَبَ بِنْ مِنْ دِيكْلَانْ وَاعْتَذَرَ. قَبِلَ دِيكْلَانْ اِعْتِذَارَهُ ، وَهُمَا الْآنَ أَصْدِقَاءٌ مَرَّةً أُخْرَى.

Story 49

High-school Feud

Declan and Ben were best friends in high school. They did everything together, they went to eat together, they took their classes together, and they even took the same route home together. Suddenly, they stopped talking after they had a dispute amongst themselves. They didn't speak to each other for over two years. Yesterday, they came across each other on the same international flight. It was awkward for both of them. They didn't say a word to each other for multiple hours until Ben approached Declan and apologized. Declan accepted his apology, and they are now friends again.

الْقِصَّةُ الْخَمْسِينَ

ضَابِطُ الشُّرْطَةِ الْمُذْنِبُ

كَانَ هُنَاكَ تَحْقِيقٌ فِيدْرَالِيٌّ جَارٍ لِقَضِيَّةِ التَّحْقِيقِ فِي جَرِيمَةِ قَتْلٍ. وَهَذِهِ الْقَضِيَّةُ مُسْتَمِرَّةٌ مُنْذُ أَكْثَرَ مِنْ عَامَيْنِ حَتَّى الْآنَ. حَتَّى هَذِهِ النُّقْطَةِ كَانَ هُنَاكَ الْقَلِيلُ مِنْ الْمَعْلُومَاتِ حَوْلَ كَيْفَ فَقَدَ الصَّبِيُّ حَيَاتَهُ. لَمْ يَكُنْ هُنَاكَ لَقَطَاتُ كَامِيرَاتِ الْمُرَاقَبَةِ ، لَا دَلِيلَ الْحَمْضِ النَّوَوِيِّ ، أَوْ أَيِّ شَيْءٍ مِنْ هَذَا النَّوْعِ. بِالْأَمْسِ ، أَبْلَغَتْ سَيِّدَةٌ مَحَلِّيَّةُ الشُّرْطَةِ بِأَنَّ أَحَدَ ضُبَّاطِ الشُّرْطَةِ كَانَ وَرَاءَ الْجَرِيمَةِ وَأَنَّهُ دَفَعَ لَهَا كَيْ تَبْقَى هَادِئَةً وَلَا تُقَدِّمَ الْأَدِلَّةُ. جَلَبَتْ كُلُّ أَدِلَّتِهَا ، تَسْجِيلٌ صَوْتِيٌّ لِضَابِطِ الشُّرْطَةِ ، وَكِيسٌ كَبِيرٌ مِنْ الْمَالِ. وَقَدْ صَدِمَتْ الْمَحْكَمَةُ بِهَذِهِ الْأَنْبَاءِ. بَعْدَ التَّحْقِيق، حُكِمَ عَلَى عَرْضِ الشُّرْطَةِ بِالسَّجْنِ مَدَى الْحَيَاةِ بِالْأَمْسِ

Story 50

The guilty police officer

There was a federal investigation ongoing for a murder investigation case. This case has been ongoing for over two years now. Up until this point, there had been very little information about how the boy lost his life. There was no CCTV footage, no DNA evidence, or anything of that sort. Yesterday, a local lady reported to the police that a police officer was behind the crime and that he paid her to remain quiet and not bring the evidence forward. She brought all of her evidence, a voice recording of the police officer, and a large bag of money. The Court was shocked by this news. Upon investigation, the police offer was sentenced to life yesterday.

My final request…

Being a smaller author, reviews help me tremendously!

It would mean the world to me if you could leave a review.

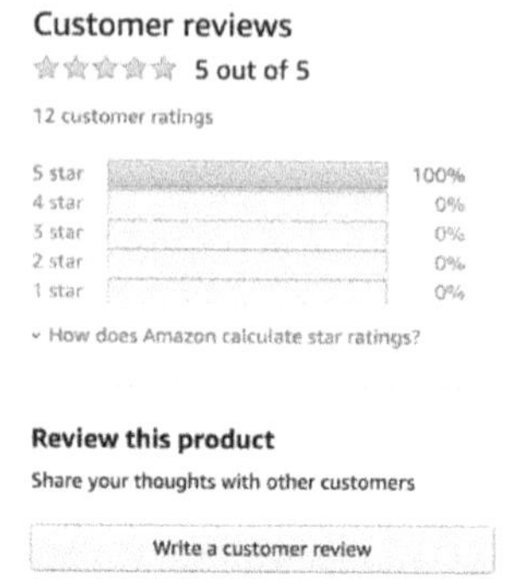

If you liked reading this book and learned a thing or two, please let me know!

It only takes 30 seconds but means so much to me!

Thank you and I can't wait to see your thought.

Conclusion

I hope you have enjoyed the stories and have managed to take out as much vocabulary and verbs from them as possible. Hopefully, by this time, you can differentiate between a verb and a noun when you come between them in texts. To further develop your study, I recommend you conjugate any new verbs that you have learned from these stories. How you can do this is by copying that verb into here:

https://conjugator.reverso.net/conjugation-english.html

What is great about this tool is that you don't need the 3rd person root verb to conjugate the verbs. All you simply do is type the verb into the search engine of the conjugator in its original form as it has come in the story, and it will do the rest of the work for you!

I also highly recommend you to buy a separate notebook and a dictionary that you will dedicate solely for the purpose of new vocabulary. Every time you come across a new word, write it down into your notebook. to further strengthen your understanding of that noun, it's recommended to learn both the singular and plural versions of it. On top of that, I would also recommend you to learn the opposite of that word. E.g., if you learned the word "Cold," I would recommend you to learn the opposite, which is "hot."

Pairing this with an Arabic language curriculum, you will find yourself very immersed in the language and reached a high level in 8-12 months. Arabic is a language all about dedication and commitment. The vast majority of people don't make it through not because of a lack of ability, rather a lack of discipline. Make sure to ride the storm during the initial struggling periods. I promise that you will overcome this hurdle and be fluent in no time, as long as you stick to it!

Resources

Presentations, B. (2012). *A Very Brief History of Storytelling - Big Fish Presentations*. Big Fish Presentations. Retrieved 13 July 2021, from https://bigfishpresentations.com/2012/02/28/a-very-brief-history-of-storytelling/.

The power of storytelling | The Health Foundation. The Health Foundation. (2016). Retrieved 13 July 2021, from https://www.health.org.uk/newsletter-feature/power-of-storytelling.

Learn A New Language With Stories – I Will Teach You A Language. I Will Teach You A Language. Retrieved 13 July 2021, from https://iwillteachyoualanguage.com/learn-language-stories.

Prins, R., Avraamidou, L., & Goedhart, M. (2017). Tell me a Story: the use of narrative as a learning tool for natural selection. *Educational Media International*, *54*(1), 20-33. https://doi.org/10.1080/09523987.2017.1324361

www.ingramcontent.com/pod-product-compliance
Ingram Content Group UK Ltd.
Pitfield, Milton Keynes, MK11 3LW, UK
UKHW022017190726
13853UKWH00005B/1986